DEVOLUTION OF POWER

Rolling Back the Federal State to Preserve the Republic

William L. Kovacs

Publishing Coordinator – Sharon Kizziah-Holmes

Paperback-Press
an imprint of A & S Publishing
Paperback Press, LLC
Springfield, Missouri

ISBN -13: 978-1-960499-79-0

DEDICATION

This book is dedicated to my very young grandson, Vireo. He did not help me in any manner with the book; however, he, his many friends, and all the young children in the United States shall inherit the many trillions in national debt the federal government is accumulating in our names. Bless these young people for our debts will place them into involuntary servitude to the federal government. Regrettably the federal government will not appreciate their struggle and will ask them to pay for more of its mismanagement.

CONTENTS

ACKNOWLEDGMENTS

Acknowledging those who helped with the book is an honor. Brandon T. Crowther of Next Level Editing, my editor, worked tirelessly to help shape the words into a compelling argument. We had a deal. I asked for as much criticism as he could give and he gave it to me. Thanks, Brandon. I should also mention Brandon edited my second book, *The Left's Little Red Book on Forming a New Green Republic*. And, Sharon Kizziah-Holmes of Paper Back Press converted a pile of papers with words on the pages into a beautifully formatted book. She performs the magic that allows everyone to read different ideas. She is an electronic Guttenberg. And of course, Jaycee DeLorenzo, Sweet and 'N Spicy Designs. To be honest, the topic of government reform is difficult to appreciate on the best of days. On its worse days, it is the book version of "Brussel sprouts." To overcome built-in resistance to the topic, authors attempt to place striking covers around their books hoping to grab the three seconds of attention given the book by browsers. Jaycee is the artist who so creatively designed the captivating cover for *Devolution of Power*. She perfectly captures the book's message by combining the design of an 18th century pamphlet with a tattered American flag.

Finally, and most fortunately, my influencer was not limited to writing 280 characters on X. His political theories would not attract much of an audience on Tik-Tok or a YouTube channel. From his portraits he looks a little like Mr. Burns, Homer Simpson's boss. With just a quill, ink and many sheets of parchment paper he developed many of the political theories that form the basis of our Constitution. He is John Locke, a 17th century political philosopher. Unfortunately, history and specifically, federal government officials have forgotten what I believe to be a most significant contribution, that no power is given to government officials as individuals. They are to serve in office as fiduciaries to protect freedom by ensuring each institution of government acts as a check on the other branches of government. I sincerely hope that this book reignites an interest in Locke's brilliant but forgotten theory.

The Author

INTRODUCTION

Devolution of Power addresses the question more than half the population of the United States thinks about but is afraid to speak about – Can our mismanaged federal government unite and govern a polarized nation? If not, how does it divide?

The hobgoblin stalking the United States is a federal government that controls a significant amount of our money, resources, and freedom. It is a collection of "elites" who lack an understanding of the needs of the nation they govern. It spends more money and enacts more programs than it can effectively manage. It rules not by trust but by imposing hundreds of thousands of laws, regulations, and taxes on us. Worse, it has created a two-tier system of justice that exempts the politically connected from its laws. Rolling back the federal state before it collapses the nation is imperative if the United States is to continue its leadership in the world.

The hostility within the nation results from the policies and rhetoric coming out of Washington and its media supporters. The powerful forces at work believe that whatever is best for them is best for the country. Compounding the division within our nation is the fact that the Progressive Left wants to dominate the actions of the conservative states. Conversely, conservative states detest the Left's wokeism and socialism. Conservatives would relish watching blue states collapse from unworkable policies.

Commentators write about solutions, including a civil war, five or more separate regions, or a divorce between red and blue states. No border compromises or separation agreements can persuade the federal government to divide the Union in any manner. It will never voluntarily give up territory without bloodshed. Like the Hotel California, states can check out any time they want; they just can't leave. Moreover, by groveling for federal dollars, states now function as paid administrators of federal programs. By accepting federal largesse that subjects them to thousands of federal dictates, the states have trapped themselves in an uncomfortable living arrangement that requires them to relinquish their sovereignty, or in essence, their souls.

Many states want their sovereignty restored but realize there is no exit from the Union or that they depend on the federal government to keep them afloat. Devolution of power is the only escape valve. Devolution of power to the states keeps the Union together by dispersing power, management, and accountability throughout the nation and more freedom for the states that want it. By having states responsible for many of the domestic policies, the federal government can focus on its most important responsibility to protect the security of the nation.

Devolving power to the states is very feasible when one understands that the U.S. federal government is not the United States, although it acts as its ruler. Instead, it is an instrumentality of the people established to manage their governmental affairs. None of our federal officials are granted power as individuals. Their duty of loyalty must be to the Constitution and the branch of government in which they serve. This separation of powers is essential to protecting the nation from tyranny. Those who place political ambition above their duty of loyalty to the

Constitution and protecting the separation of powers in government, violate their sacred oath.

Unfortunately, since the creation of the federal government, the individuals acquiring federal power have skillfully blended the powers of the three federal branches into two competing power structures not established by the Constitution. These power structures are called political parties. As such, citizens are not protected by the Constitution; they are only protected by Democrats or Republicans, depending on which party controls the apparatus of government.

As crucial as right-sizing the federal government, is the need to find competent, trustworthy people to manage it. Citizens need to elect officials that will serve as trustees of the Constitution they have sworn to protect and fiduciaries to the institutions in which they serve. By giving all loyalty to the Constitution, and the institution in which they serve, every official will be a constant check on the power of the federal government.

Devolution of Power provides a roadmap for establishing a rational governing structure for the nation. The new governing structure will free the federal government from the many responsibilities it has accumulated but is incapable of managing. Such freedom will allow the federal government to focus on protecting the nation. Moreover, by devolving many of the domestic functions to the states, citizens will be governed by smaller, more efficient, and accountable governments offering services citizens want and can afford rather than those mandated by the federal government.

PART I

Can the U.S. Unite? If Not, How Does It Divide?

CHAPTER 1

The Federal Government Is Not the United States, It Is a Governing Mechanism that Can Be Changed

The federal government is the central governmental body in the U.S. It is *not* the United States. Instead, it is a constitutionally established mechanism in which representatives of the people are granted temporary, limited powers to advance the nation's common good. These representatives are not given individual or personal powers. They are to serve as trustees of the Constitution and fiduciaries who owe their duty of loyalty to the institution in which they serve.

Their loyalty to the institution in which they serve is part of the Constitution's infrastructure that protects liberty by requiring each institution to continuously operate as a check on the power of the other branches of government. These checks are essential since the framework of our Constitution has few guardrails as to the type of government the individuals controlling it can create. As long as the people are able to elect a government to make laws somewhat in accordance with a very broad and vague Constitution, it is a constitutionally permissible U.S. government. Our federal government could function as capitalist, socialist, oligarchy, kakistocracy, woke cult, or as a "deep secretive intelligence state" that poses as a Republic. Today the U.S. is a mix of these governing mechanisms.

While the nation's people elect representatives to Congress with the theoretical mandate to work for the common good, the nation's political culture prevents Congress and the other branches of government from achieving this goal. Today our elected representatives and government officials are more loyal to the political party that helped them secure their jobs than to the institution in which they serve.

If members of Congress gave all their loyalty to the institution of Congress and protected the Constitution, Congress would be a continuous check on the increasing power of the executive and judicial branches. If such a check had been functioning for the last century, the nation would not be at financial risk, with open borders, and a massive regulatory state with a two-tier justice system. The people of the U.S. no longer trust the federal government and for good reason.

By giving more loyalty to political parties than the institution they serve, our government officials have *de facto* changed our Constitution from one in which three constitutionally established institutions of government protect our liberties, to one in which we are only protected by Republicans or Democrats, depending on who is in power. The individuals occupying federal positions have assumed such tremendous personal power that they have become the rulers. We, the people, have become their servants.

Fortunately, the ultimate power under our Constitution is the right of citizens every two years to elect a new House of Representatives and one-third of the Senate. Our right to vote is the power to bring about revolutionary change every two years. It is a power that allows citizens to choose the type of government they want to live under. It is time citizens recognize that when the institutions of government fail to protect their liberties, they have the power to change that government. With such deep citizen distrust of the federal government, it is time to limit its powers. Devolving federal power to the states is merely a workable mechanism for controlling excessive federal power.

CHAPTER 2

An Empire on the Edge of Collapse

History tells cruel stories. Complex societies collapse. Massively indebted nations collapse. Countries with their military deployed throughout the world collapse. Highly regulated countries collapse. Governments that are torn by distrust and hatred between many factions collapse. The United States is all of these risks combined while its federal government arrogantly sits on the edge of collapse, believing itself immortal.

The federal government deludes itself thinking that it can't happen here. It has happened to every major empire in the history of the world. Nothing is written that the U.S. is eternal.

History is littered with collapsed empires. The world power centers of the 16th and 17th centuries included the Spanish, Portuguese and Ottoman empires. In the 18th century it was the British empire. In the 19th century, the great empires were French, Austro-Hungarian, Italian, German, Russian and British. All these countries were substantially diminished by some combination of war, excessive centralization, debt, distrust, or a failure to adapt technology to changing times. None are great powers today.

Like all empires before us, our society will live with the risk government has created, perhaps for decades, but then some sudden event will force dramatic change, and our government will be helpless to address it. At that point, the entire society may decline or, at times, drift into the abyss. Once the decline starts, it can take decades or even centuries to reverse it.

There are times in the history of nations when the citizens of the nation need to act before those entrusted with the control and resources of the nation cause it harm. Now is the time for action!

Today the United States is in a state of unreason, the absence of reason, or simply insanity. Political decisions are made to enhance power, punish enemies, and separate Americans into opposing camps. Such a state of unreason clouds the judgment of those who run our government. Unreason drains the nation's collective soul of the ability to communicate with each other and the government.

The federal government uses language to make us believe something other than its true intent or facts. A crisis is called an opportunity. Censorship is called free speech. Allowing millions of illegal immigrants that include drug cartels and human traffickers into the country is considered a humanitarian gesture. Giving trillions of dollars to private supporters of the government is considered building infrastructure.

Justice before the law benefits those with power and connections. Friends of a current government are free to violate the law. Radical groups that support the forces of government are allowed to burn cities. These "peaceful protesters" are exercising their rights to free speech and their conduct offers the president an opportunity to "Build Back Better."

Individuals the federal government finds objectionable are enemies of the state. They are criminals and their homes can be raided and their lives destroyed by endless prosecutions. While the United States has the most prisoners in the world, it now adds a new class of prisoners – political prisoners, a category usually found in totalitarian regimes.

Radicals want to "cancel" Abraham Lincoln, George Washington, and even Dr. Seuss for being racists. Many of our public schools fight to conceal from parents what is being taught to their children. Curriculums are being dumbed down so poor performing students feel equal to those who can read, write, and do mathematics at grade level or above. Teachers spend more time teaching politically correct pronouns than the best literature. Parents of these children who object to this woke education are deemed domestic terrorists and threatened by the Federal Bureau of Investigation ("FBI").

Our federal investigative agencies are so corrupt they flagrantly file false reports with the courts to take down political opponents. And the courts, out of fear or stupidity, accept the reports and authorize the illegal activities. The federal government, in the name of privacy, hides information that might shed light on its crimes while allowing its many spy agencies and big tech to track our every movement, listen to our every word, read our every keystroke on a computer, and determine the "truth" we hear and read. It has recently been revealed the FBI even spied on congressional investigators who were investigating the FBI.

The federal government so drained the nation's financial resources that it will soon be unable to pay its bills. Our $34 trillion national debt is so large, our children will be in *de facto,* involuntary servitude to the federal government. The federal government lacks a plan to manage its debt, live within its means, or ensure our tax money is spent on the nation's real needs.

Compounding matters, the federal government uses our money to bribe the respective states to implement federal programs. Now many states are addicted to federal handouts and serve as administrators to the federal government, notwithstanding that the states are merely receiving a portion of the money *their citizens* send to Washington.

Fear is the mood of the nation. Many citizens acting together have the power to stop the madness, but they remain silent. The government officials who speak loudly speak only for personal gain. Lincoln warned us that "a house divided cannot stand." We uncomfortably live in that house.

Where does the United States go from here?

A civil war will only bring more unreason and violent repression. The Progressive commentators who despise conservative thought frequently discuss civil war, not as a means to prevent it, but as a justification for attacking or jailing political opponents. Before any irreversible actions occur, a path must be found that allows those deemed "objectionable" citizens to find freedom from a growing mob that is a mix of the federal government, big business, cancel culture, Progressive radicals, and the political left. Finding freedom from the mob will be difficult since it is obsessed with dominating those it deems "objectionable."

The mob will fight as hard as possible to prevent any "objectionable" from escaping the federal government's rule.

The underlying conditions in the nation will likely force radical change in the federal government, no matter what the federal government wants. The federal government may believe it can defend the country from enemies. Our enemies, however, will not forget the U.S. disastrously retreating from Viet Nam and Afghanistan, Russia taking Crimea, China crushing Hong Kong, the wind blowing away several red lines in the sand in Syria, and Iran daring the world to respond to it flagrantly building a nuclear arsenal. The federal government is unable even to protect U.S. sovereignty from a Chinese spy balloon or the millions of illegal immigrants, foreign terrorists, drug cartels, and sex traffickers illegally crossing our southern border.

Cyber-attacks on federal government computers, our telecommunications, and energy infrastructure are merely tests to determine how large an attack must be to dominate a bankrupt, divided, and militarily-weakened U.S.

Our federal government believes it has control of the nation. At the same time, it depends on China for the basic materials and products needed to run our country, including pharmaceuticals, technology, manufactured products, and the rare earth materials required for its green economy. We have hundreds of billions a year in trade deficits with China, an economy that will soon be the largest on earth. Its military is brutally suppressing freedom. It controls the South China Sea and threatens the nations in that region so they "stay in line." Now China has a spy post in Cuba, ninety miles off our shore, along with Russia. The U.S. response is to have its "leaders" pontificate on cable television and send our enemies "strong letters" of objection.

China builds economic development and trade relations with over 130 countries through its Belt and Road Initiative. Our generals testify to Congress that the greatest threat to our country is domestic, far-right, white extremists. These same generals minimize threats from Iran, China, Russia, and North Korea while teaching Critical Race Theory at West Point.

We have a president that utters nonsense and cannot read his talking points from a teleprompter. Yet, he limits the nation's energy production when the world is in desperate need of energy resources.

Satisfaction with public life in America has plunged to 39%. Only 27% of Americans are satisfied with our system of government, down from 43% the year before. Only 18% of Americans are satisfied with our morals and ethics, down from 32% the prior year.

The federal government has separated itself from its citizens. Government functions primarily for its own benefit. While most citizens want to live peaceful lives with family and community, the federal government asserts it is not accountable to citizens. It has sovereign immunity, "it can do no wrong." Other than voting a corrupt government out of office, citizens cannot challenge government corruption since the executive determines what is corruption. The political parties protect corrupt presidents from conviction if impeached and make calling a Constitutional Convention impossible. The only constant power Congress has to challenge the outrageous actions of the federal government is the power of the purse. Unfortunately, Congress only uses this power to expand the federal government. It has not used its power of the purse to reduce government since World War II.

The political theories underlying our Constitution hold that government is by the consent of the people. However, as discussed in chapter 7, almost from the instant the federal government was formed, Congress, the president and the U.S. Supreme Court began expanding federal powers. The executive covets congressionally delegated powers while the courts rubberstamp new federal powers. Congress has delegated away so many of its powers to the president and executive branch agencies over the years that it has made itself generally dysfunctional. As congressional power shrinks, the president restructures the federal government by claiming the authority to determine the freedom of citizens and the use of the nation's resources.

The practical tipping point, however, that will send the United States into the abyss is the federal government's obsession with climate change. The federal government provides trillions in subsidies to the green technology industry that depends on China for the minerals needed to make its products. All of this unreason is based upon a belief that the planet will be destroyed if the nation does not quickly eliminate the use of fossil fuels. The federal government's climate policies are so blind that it does not recognize that almost every product made, nearly all transportation, housing, commercial buildings, and our infrastructure, depends on fossil fuels. Without fossil fuels, there will be no nation to save. Worse, however, is that an all-electric economy is an all-digital economy that can be easily attacked and shut down by almost any government that employs sophisticated hackers.

If the federal government continues with its current policies, it will travel a path taken by China in 1433, when it was the ruler of the seas. It had great wealth from international trade. However, China's political elite were so obsessed and fearful of international trade and the rise of the mercantile class that they intentionally destroyed the foundation of their wealth, their great sailing fleets.

China, like the U.S. today, was in a state of unreason. The seventh voyage of China's Treasure Fleet returned home. The Fleet was under the command of Admiral Zheng He. The seven voyages of the Fleet took the ships to the Indian Ocean, Asia, the Arabian Peninsula, and the Horn of Africa. There were up to 3,500 ships in the Fleet, some as long as 400 feet and 160 feet wide, and with nine masts. For comparison, the current U.S. Navy only has 162 ships and 68 submarines.

The seventh voyage was undertaken with over 100 large ships and 27,000 men. The treasure ships returned home to hostile political division. The Mandarins (bureaucrats) and the eunuchs (the merchant class) were political enemies. The Mandarins were concerned that the merchant class was becoming too rich and influential from international trade. During the seventh voyage, the emperor who funded the great expeditions died, and his grandson became emperor. Also, the leader of the voyage, Admiral He, died on the seventh voyage. When the Fleet returned to China, the new emperor ordered the Fleet grounded. Many of the ships were burned, and others were allowed to rot. All international trade was forbidden. Around 1477, the Ministry of War confiscated and destroyed all of Admiral He's records. The records were labeled "deceitful exaggerations of bizarre things far removed from the testimony of people's eyes and ears." By 1525, China limited all ships to two masts and ordered the destruction of all ocean-going vessels. These events were the initial catalyst of China's slide into poverty for almost five-hundred years.

Many politicians today, like the Mandarins, want to use raw, arbitrary power to destroy the very aspects of our society that generate wealth. The Mandarins destroyed the ships that brought them wealth. Today, many in the federal government and its advocacy groups seek to destroy what makes us great: the rule of law, free speech, free enterprise, and affordable energy from fossil fuels. Since regulating the climate can capture every aspect of society, a federal climate change policy allows the federal government to totally control all human conduct, including the food we eat, the type and amount of the energy we use, all forms of transportation, the products we can buy and the size of the homes we live in. The imposition of tyranny requires such control. Regulating climate changes gives the federal government the power to control all of society.

The story of 1433 is a cautionary tale. If we don't remember it, we may be handing global dominance back to China as the federal government drives the United States into centuries of darkness and poverty.

CHAPTER 3

The Hostile Takeover of the Federal Government by the Two Major Political Parties

The U.S. Constitution formed a government based on the consent of the people. It was to be a government of limited powers. Each branch was to serve as a check on the other branches. Only by each branch of government constantly checking the powers of the other branches can a limited government be maintained and freedom secured.

Those serving in government are not given power as individuals. Their power is as representatives of the people. Their responsibility is to defending the Constitution and giving their loyalty to the branch they serve. Unfortunately, those serving in government today operate as the factions Madison feared would destroy the Republic. In Federalist Paper 10, he defined a faction as "A number of citizens, whether amounting to a minority or majority of the whole, who are united and actuated by some common impulse of passion or interest, adverse to the rights of other citizens or to the permanent and aggregate interests of the community." Today, factions have organized as political parties, to capture the federal government for personal power. They have destroyed the majestic intentions of our Constitution.

The Republican and Democratic parties ("R&D parties"), using their combined power as a monopoly over who serves in government, have so manipulated the election laws of the nation that they have complete and permanent control over who runs government at all levels of the United States. These political parties have amassed almost total government control without being established by, or even mentioned in, the Constitution. The R&D parties secured their control by enacting election laws that substantially favor their candidates while imposing discriminatory and burdensome requirements on all third-party competitors.

The R&D parties are nothing more than highly organized, demographically diverse, not-for-profit, advocacy groups of individuals. They use a corporate structure to organize nationally. The sole purpose of the R&D parties is to control all levels of government in the United States by electing their members to positions in government.

People think of monopolies in a corporate sense—one business having exclusive control over a part of our economy through legal privilege or concerted illegal action. Monopolistic control limits competition. There are laws restricting the anti-competitive activities of corporations.

In the political world, however, those having majority control of federal and state legislatures, the R&D parties, have the power to enact laws to ensure their members almost always win every election. Controlling who wins political office directly translates into the type of laws passed, which citizens or corporations receive government benefits, who is taxed more or less, how commerce is regulated, and who will judge us should we violate any of the laws enacted by the R&D controlled legislatures.

The statistics demonstrating the R&D parties' control are stunning. In her book, *Becoming a Candidate*, Jennifer Lawless counts 519,682 elected officeholders in the United States. Of this total, the Libertarian Party, in 2017, claimed 168 of these officeholders; the Green Party in 2016 held 143 offices, and the Constitution Party held 12 offices. Many of these positions are non-partisan offices. There were also at least 29 Independent officeholders, including 3 U.S. Senators who caucus with the Democrats and 26 Democratic Vermont Progressives. A basic calculation places the third-party competitors' share of elected officials nationwide at 0.0007254%. Conversely, the R&D parties' control 99.99% of the elected offices in the U.S.

The R&D parties ruthlessly maintain their political control by imposing burdensome requirements on third-party candidates and filing costly lawsuits challenging the signatures on the petitions of third-party candidates to drain the scarce resources of small parties.

Professor Brian Porto, in his law review article, "The Constitution and the Ballot Box," explains that while political parties were organized a few years after the founding of our country, it was not until the 1912 elections, when Teddy Roosevelt's Bull Moose party received more votes than the Republicans, that the two major parties and their elected federal, state and local officials feared they needed protection from new political parties. In the 1912 election, the Socialist Party received six percent of the presidential vote and won several congressional seats, 79 mayoralties, and over 1,200 local offices. As fear gripped the R&D parties, state legislatures began making access to the ballot more difficult for third-party candidates to challenge R&D candidates.

Examples of roadblocks imposed on third-party candidates:

- Requiring a significant number of signatures, e.g., 3% of the vote in the last Gubernatorial race, while waiving or substantially reducing the number of signatures needed by R&D party candidates;
- Providing shorter time periods for third-party candidates to gather signatures than for R&D party candidates;
- Requiring third-party presidential nominees to file nominating petitions eight months before the election and months before the R&D party candidates had to file;
- Imposing signature distribution requirements on third-party candidates, e.g., a certain number of signatures from each county or congressional district; and
- Requiring new third parties to nominate candidates for every office up for election in that cycle.

Each obstacle to ballot access by other political parties was an intentional act to limit political competition. By limiting political competition, the R&D parties guarantee perpetual control of all government in the U.S.

The primary arguments for limiting ballot access are that it promotes political stability and reduces unrestrained factionalism and voter confusion. Unfortunately, the R&D parties have failed miserably to promote political stability or reduce factions as evidenced by the nation's massive national debt, its many undeclared wars, a decades long failure to enact appropriations to fund government, and uncompromising extreme factions. Moreover, since the two major parties are controlled by small groups of extremely vocal advocates, a majority of Americans have lost trust in the political process.

The real downside, however, to eliminating political competition is that it eliminates new ideas for solving contentious political problems. In essence, the R&D parties fundamentally changed the structure of the Constitution of the U.S. from one in which three independent institutions of government were to check the powers of each other, to one in which Republicans and Democrats control the institutions of government to achieve power for their party. This change is dramatic. Federal power is no longer limited by constitutionally established institutions. The only limits on federal power are those that can be imposed by Republican or Democratic rulers.

CHAPTER 4

States Check into the U.S.A. Under Hotel California Rules

When states join the United States, they check in under the rules of the Hotel California: "*You [states] can check-out anytime you like, but you can never leave!*" No matter how bad it gets! No matter how much the state is diminished or its citizens threatened, it can never leave! The principles of the Declaration of Independence be damned! Moreover, states receive so much federal money, they have transformed themselves into administrators of federal programs. As state sovereignty is diluted, states are less able to protect their citizens. The federal government's open southern border policy exemplifies why Texas and Arizona cannot protect their citizens against arbitrary federal rule.

Every empire has broken apart by internal conflict, unmanageable debt, or war since humans organized. While there is no set timeframe for a nation's longevity, it is very likely, however, that at some point, there will be a set of circumstances that will serve as a catalyst to tear the U.S. apart. One piece of wise guidance on avoiding civil war comes from an unexpected source, Grand Duke Mikhailovich, in a letter to the last Tsar of Russia in 1917. As disorganization and lawlessness manifested themselves throughout Russia, he wrote:

A situation like this cannot last long. I repeat once more – It is impossible to rule the country without paying attention to the voice of the people, without meeting their needs, without a willingness to admit that the people themselves understand their own needs.

Heeding the Grand Duke's warning was very difficult for a czar. It is equally as difficult for a federal government that demands total control over a nation. While following such advice requires listening to the people, it also requires enough luck for the compromise process to work before the country breaks apart. The writer Hunter S. Thompson noted: *Luck is a very thin wire between survival and disaster, and not many people [or governments] can keep their balance on it.* The U.S. is wobbly on that very thin wire. There is significant distrust and overwhelming disapproval of the federal government's propaganda and media misinformation organizations. If this nation wants to save itself from a potential breakup, it must, within the time it has, find a compromise that allows all citizens, even those it finds objectionable, to live in freedom with a government that respects that freedom.

The federal government, call it the ruling class, oligarchs, the kakistocracy, deep state, or just out-of-touch rulers and media moguls, finds millions of Americans "objectionable." These Americans are non-big city, religious, rural, and working-class people. Hillary Clinton characterizes them as a "basket of deplorables" holding "racist, sexist, homophobic, xenophobic, Islamophobic" views.

Former President Barack Obama characterized these objectionable Americans as: "… bitter, they cling to guns or religion or antipathy toward people who aren't like them or anti-immigrant sentiment." A recent tweet by a New York Times reporter identified these objectionable Americans as "legitimate national security threats" and "enemies of the state."

The views of Clinton, Obama, and the New York Times about Americans who act in ways they do not condone, are shared throughout the ruling, monied, DC, Hollywood, socialist, academic classes, and the federal bureaucracy. Their views sanction a disdain that allows these elites to believe they are superior, in knowledge and culture, to the ordinary people who want to live in peace. This superiority complex is the fundamental reason the ruling class is comfortable censoring objectionable speech and freeing violent criminals to commit more crimes against ordinary people. The ruling class does not value ordinary people.

The federal government and its elite friends, with their personal security and private jets, demand the objectionable Americans submit to their "utopian beliefs" that, when implemented, impose costly and authoritarian mandates on ordinary Americans. These elites want more than determining the cars Americans drive, the energy they use, and what appliances can be in their homes. They want to be free to do whatever they want while having the power to control the lives of ordinary citizens, starting with what is taught to our children.

Finding a structure that allows the diverse beliefs of the blue and red states in the Union to live in peace requires asking whether there is enough flexibility in the Constitution to keep the Union together. Under the U.S. Supreme Court's decision in *Texas v. White,* an 1868 case determining the status of Texas after the Civil War, the Supreme Court held that the United States is an indestructible Union composed of indestructible states.

According to the *White* Court, change in the structure of the Union can only occur through revolution or the consent of the states. The federal government and its massive and overwhelming military power make it impossible for any state to leave its control without its approval. President Biden made this point very clear when he quipped, "If you wanted or if you think you need to have weapons to take on the government, you need F-15s and maybe some nuclear weapons." Anyone challenging the federal government should take Biden's statement as the threat it is. After the January 6th riots at the Capitol, the real danger to the "objectionable" citizen could be imprisonment for decades for participating in whatever the federal government deems to be an "insurrection."

Moreover, it is highly improbable the red states would ever secure the consent of a sufficient number of blue states to exit the Union since it is the continued growth of the federal government that is the goal of the blue states.

Breaking away from the Union is merely wishful thinking. There is always that unhappy portion of any place in the USA. Some writers claim parts of the U.S. have wanted to split since its inception. These writers have a complete revisionist history of the U.S. by asserting there was dissent from the beginning. In the aftermath of Brexit, these writers held false hope of the U.S. undergoing a Brexit experience. They speculated about future Republics in Texas, California, or Vermont. They dubbed them, Texit, Calexit, and Verexit. The basis for such hope rests with Texas and California being independent Republics and Vermont being an independent state before becoming part of the Union. Once these states voluntarily joined the Union, the prospect of a no-fault separation was buried in a big dust-heap of history.

Under this narrow reading of *White*, it appears the two Americas must live together no matter how poorly they get along or how badly the federal government treats ordinary Americans or several of its states. But then there was the collapse of the USSR in 1991. So, one never knows when a nation will lose its balance on that very thin wire. Fortunately, the Supreme Court in *White* offers a ray of hope.

The court notes, "But the perpetuity and indissolubility of the Union by no means implies the loss of distinct and individual existence, or of the right of self-government by the States." The critical point is that states have the right to self-government within the indissoluble Union. This more liberal reading of *White* offers a path for the two Americas to live in harmony. Since *White* holds that states never lose their distinct and individual right of self-government and Article IV of the Constitution mandates the federal government guarantee every state a Republican form of government, the Supreme Court provides an opening for compromise. Devolution of power is a compromise that allows red and blue states to be governed under domestic laws that fit the beliefs of their citizens while the federal government protects the United States from its enemies.

In the final analysis the likelihood of any structural changes to the Union will be determined by who controls the federal government. Politicians seeking power over all aspects of the nation will manage the nation far differently than citizens who serve in office as trustees of the Constitution and fiduciaries to the institution in which they serve. Politicians run government for their personal benefit and that of their political parties and friends. Trustees and Fiduciaries manage government for the benefit of the people by respecting the principles of separation of powers between the branches of government and between the federal government and the states. When one branch of government checks the powers of the other branches, it protects our Constitution and the freedom of its people.

If citizens want freedom, they have no other choice but to use every ounce of energy they possess to restrain a federal government that seeks unlimited power over the people it rules.

CHAPTER 5

Can the U.S. Unite? If Not, How Does it Divide?

E very aspect of U.S. society is getting more polarized. Politicians tear at each other. The news media and social media are divided between fake news, lies, and propaganda. Our institutions, including religious institutions, are no longer trusted. The federal government's spending makes the French Queen Marie Antoinette look like a conservative money manager. For a century and a half, the federal government has expanded its powers by diminishing the standing in the Union of the sovereign states. Most Americans are exhausted by politics.

It's time to ask the question - What do the people think about this conflict? After all, it is suppositively their country.

A Rasmussen survey found 62% of voters do not believe the government spends money wisely. Only 25% believe the government is careful in how it spends taxpayer money. A recent Gallup poll comparing trust in our institutions between 2021 and 2022 found that Americans lost trust in every institution. Trust in the president suffered the greatest loss, 15%. The U.S. Supreme Court was next with an 11% loss of trust. Big business, television news, and Congress had the lowest levels of trust overall: 14%, 11%, and 7%, respectively. Gallup has been measuring the level of trust in American institutions since 1973, and these findings are its lowest levels of trust.

Gallup found only two institutions, small businesses and the military, having the trust of a majority of Americans.

These 2023 survey results track other recent results:

- Pew Research Center finds only two in ten Americans believe they can trust the government in Washington to do what is right "just about always" (2%) or most of the time (19%). Trust in government is down from 75% in 1958.
- Gallup finds an overall lack of trust in American institutions: only 14% of Americans have a "great deal" or "quite a lot" of confidence in the criminal justice system; 16% in newspapers; and 37% in religious institutions. 84% of Americans believe media is to blame for our political divide.
- Rasmussen finds 59% of likely voters believe members of Congress care more about what the media thinks is more important than what the voters think.
- Rasmussen finds 58% of voters agree media is the "Enemy of the People."
- A survey by the Reuters Institute for the Study of Journalism found the U.S. ranks last of 46 nations in media trust, at 29% trust.

- A Public Agenda/USA Today/Ipsos poll found 90% of Americans "…are sick and tired of being so divided."
- Rassmussen finds only 37% of likely voters think the country is heading in the right direction.
- Pew Research Center finds that within states there is almost complete division over policy matters between rural and urban areas.
- Pew Research Center finds two-thirds of Americans are "worn out" by the amount of political news.
- Even within states, the conservative parts of Oregon want to join Idaho, and parts of northern California want to separate from the rest of California and form a new state.

The Georgetown University Institute of Politics and Public Service Civility Survey describes voters across all demographics as believing political, racial and class divisions are deteriorating. While it also found 80% of voters want the political parties to seek compromise and common ground, the average American voter believes the U.S. is two-thirds of the way "to the edge of a civil war."

One insight from the Georgetown survey is key to understanding why Americans think as they do. It found "a strong correlation between where people get information and how they view key issues and figures." For example, Fox News viewers have a favorable/unfavorable rating of 17/78 for Black Lives Matter. Non-Fox viewers, however, have a 59/35 favorable/unfavorable rating. Dr. Anthony Fauci has a favorable/unfavorable rating of 20/69 among Fox viewers and a 64/27 favorable/unfavorable rating among non-Fox viewers. The news channel one watches seems to broadcast the truth to the viewers.

A February 2023 Gallup/Knight Foundation poll confirms Americans do not trust the media or at least the media watched by those they disagree with. Only 26% of Americans have a positive view of the media. 50% of Americans believe the national media intends to mislead, and only 26% of Americans believe the media works in the public interest. A May 2023 AP poll finds three-quarters of Americans believe the media increases polarization in the nation.

The polling is overwhelming that Americans do not trust their institutions. A strong underlying reason for their distrust is media bias. The media uses its vast resources to intentionally divide the nation to achieve the agenda of the political party it supports. The media no longer delivers the news and needed information; instead, it is an active participant in politics. In fact, based on delivering the messages of the political parties, the media, operating under the protection of the First Amendment, is the most effective special interest/lobbying group in the nation.

A synthesis of the many polls would conclude the American people want their government to work together on matters impacting their day-to-day lives but are willing to accept conflict on non-bread-and-butter social issues. Unfortunately, due to the symbiotic relationship between media and politicians, there can never be compromise since both groups believe they have too much to gain from polarization. The result is constant conflict and the inability of the government to work for the people it is to serve. The American people are smart; they recognize this fact. 62% of voters believe neither of the two major parties adequately represents them.

Congress, the federal government, and the media are adversarial to citizens. Politicians and the media set the policy. Citizens are merely commodities that pay taxes so the politicians and the media can live well on their money.

Without trust in their institutions, it is difficult for average Americans to believe in America.

If citizens sincerely believe what they tell the pollsters, why don't they use their votes to change the system? If institutions want to be trusted, why don't they serve the purposes they were established for? If the media wants to be trusted, why doesn't it report the news accurately and fairly and let its bias come out on the opinion pages? All leads to the existential question – does anyone care about the future of the United States?

Perhaps the answers to these questions are clear and right in front of our eyes. The two major parties have monopoly control over who is elected and have made it impossible for citizens to elect officials who will serve the Constitution. The officials running our institutions care more about power than the betterment of the nation. The media cares more about advocating for management's beliefs and corporate profits than it does about accurate reporting on the activities of government.

If the U.S. cannot unite; how does it divide? The U.S. Constitution, laws, regulations, an intertwined and complex economy and banking system, controlled by the federal government, along with an overwhelming military force, makes separation improbable. Finding a way to roll back the federal state before it collapses the nation is similar to finding a way out of a mythical labyrinth. It is a journey to the center of constitutional thought to again find the soul of the United States.

PART II

The Four Horseman of the Federal Apocalypse

CHAPTER 6

First Horseman, Lawlessness

By *de facto*, abandoning the rule of law, the federal government has made itself the master and citizens its servants.

The arbitrary application of the rule of law creates deep concern within the citizenry over the future stability of the nation. Compounding this problem, the national Congress, the constitutionally established lawmaker, is generally so dysfunctional it is unable to provide the needed oversight of the executive branch.

The president and Congress have created this situation by giving their loyalty to the political party that helped elect them rather than to the institution in which they serve. As such, they achieve political goals which are illustrated by the 90% adherence to party-line voting in Congress on major legislation and the unified protection of a president's unconstitutional acts by members of Congress from his party.

When Congress is unable to check the powers of the

president, the president is able to expand its governing role from executing the laws into making laws by regulation and Executive Order. It also provides presidents with the discretion to ignore laws they dislike such as Biden's refusal to control the southern border of the U.S. This *de facto* political structure governs the nation and will remain the governing structure as long as presidents are protected by members of their political party in Congress.

This lawlessness is simple to explain. It occurs when members of Congress are of the same party as the president and give blind allegiance to his every wish, notwithstanding the unconstitutionality of his actions. By functioning as politicians, not fiduciaries, these members fail to defend the separation of powers structure of the Constitution, which is the primary check on federal power.

Even when the president's party controls only one house of Congress, the members of the president's party can allow the president to be a supreme lawmaker by blocking the actions of the minority that attempt to check the unconstitutional accumulation of power. And, when the president and both houses of Congress are controlled by the same political party, the rule of law is what the president mandates.

While unlawful Executive Orders and regulations can be challenged in the courts, it takes years to achieve any resolution of a dispute. Moreover, when a president's abuse of law is protected by his party's control of one or both houses of Congress, the president's rule is absolute since he controls the Department of Justice ("DOJ"), which determines who is or is not criminally prosecuted and which congressional subpoenas will be enforced.

Scholars pontificate on the brilliance of the separation of powers in our Constitution as a means by which each branch of the federal government checks the powers of the other branches. Notwithstanding such pontificating, the U.S. Constitution is merely a piece of paper unless every member of Congress makes it work by serving as a fiduciary to the institution of Congress, and not as a political handmaiden to the president.

The rule of law is not a rule or a law.

To have citizens believe we live in a rule-of-law society, they are taught we are all equal before the law, including government officials. This concept is described in many ways, such as "the law is the king," "no man is above the law," or "we are a government of laws, not men."

We are taught these concepts, so we believe our federal government will be fair to us. Moreover, if a member of our federal government breaks the law, it will receive the same treatment under our legal system as any lawbreaker, a very comforting concept to the naïve. The "rule of law" is not a law of any kind. It is not part of our Constitution and has no binding effect on anything. It is merely a clever phrase or, more appropriately, a fable repeated to us to make government sound fair and accountable while persuading citizens to obey its every command.

Other than the undefined, vague limits placed on the federal government by the Constitution and laws passed by Congress, there is scant mention of how our legal system applies to the operation of government when it acts illegally, even tyrannically. The federal government is not held accountable other than its members occasionally being voted out of office. It operates for its own benefit. The doctrine of sovereign immunity protects those running government from being subjected to citizens seeking recourse against it for unlawful actions or even crimes.

Sovereign immunity is not written into our Constitution.

Sovereign immunity is merely a doctrine the U.S. Supreme Court recognized 90 years after the ratification of our Constitution. While the Supreme Court protects federal power by applying the doctrine, it struggles with a definitive foundation for using it. The doctrine currently holds that the federal government cannot be sued without its consent. It bars all lawsuits against the federal government or its officers unless Congress enacts a law expressing its intent to lift the bar. With *de facto* immunity from suit, unless otherwise legislated, there are few mechanisms to hold the United States government and its officials accountable for their actions. The government waives immunity from suit in civil actions, such as torts, breach of contract, copyright violations, tax disputes, open records laws, and civil rights violations when government officials are acting under the color of law. The government sets out specific procedures for making these claims and limits a citizen's recovery to monetary damages or injunctive relief. The Government Accountability Office, however, clearly notes the waiver of sovereign immunity is not enough to assume the victim will be compensated. Legally, there can be no payment without a congressional appropriation.

While Congress for decades has had in place the Court of Federal Claims and the Judgment Fund to generally ensure monetary payments to successful litigants, sovereign immunity prohibits citizens from taking action against the federal government for criminal activity. As such, the federal government is free to prosecute its enemies at the time of its choosing and allow criminals committing crimes on its behalf to roam free. The contrast between the lack of prosecution of Hunter Biden and the use of the entire federal government and a few states to prosecute former President Trump is a clear illustration of the federal government's arbitrary application of the law.

Since the federal government is immune from liability unless it authorizes suit against itself or the corrupt government prosecutes itself, an unlikely scenario, a citizen's only recourse is to vote the corrupt government out of office. That process takes time. The Constitution provides the quicker and more direct approach if another branch of government checks the powers of the corrupt or abusive branch. Congress can control an abusive branch by impeachment proceedings or reducing or eliminating appropriations that fund the abusive conduct. Courts could enjoin the corrupt conduct; however, such an order is only as powerful as the court, which has no enforcement powers if the DOJ resists. Traditionally, the DOJ had respect for court orders; now it is willing to lie to the courts to further its righteousness. This breakdown in the rule of law is a sign of a life-threatening disease in our government.

Other examples of the federal government's abuse of law.

Example One of federal government corruption is when Congress issued a subpoena to the DOJ for information on its false filings before the Foreign Intelligence Surveillance Court ("FISA Court"). The DOJ refused to provide Congress with the documents to avoid embarrassment and likely the acknowledgment of its criminal activity. Since the DOJ is the primary law enforcement department for congressional investigators, when it refuses to provide Congress with requested documents or to prosecute itself for its unlawful acts, it destroys the ability of Congress to fulfill its constitutional role of checking the power of the Executive.

Example Two concerns the FBI forcing private companies to act illegally. The FBI regularly demanded Twitter, a private company, to ban what it deemed misinformation concerning the president's son's laptop, notwithstanding that the FBI knew the information about the president's son was true. While these actions violate the First Amendment rights of citizens and perhaps constitute direct election interference, the president will never prosecute itself or its corrupt agents carrying out its demands.

Example Three illustrates how the federal government acts as a tyrant to average citizens lacking political connections. A Navy officer took photographs of a nuclear submarine he worked on and was imprisoned for improperly handling national security secrets. During the same period, a presidential candidate, Hillary Clinton, of the same party as the sitting president destroyed, using BleachBit, significant amounts of national security materials on an unauthorized home computer. She also destroyed similar information on her cell phone by using a hammer. The candidate was never prosecuted.

Example Four contrasts the lack of prosecution of Hilary Clinton to the fact that DOJ and Democrat state prosecutors viewed Donald Trump to be an insurrectionist and an enemy of Democracy. DOJ brought prosecutions against Trump in the Florida and DC federal courts. Local Democratic prosecutors in New York and Georgia indicted Trump in state courts. The Attorney General of New York campaigned on "getting Trump." In total the prosecutors brought four indictments alleging 91 violations of criminal law against Trump as he was running for president against President Biden. No matter how negative one may think of Trump, prosecutions based on "Get Trump" are, as Professor Dershowitz asserts, a significant threat to civil liberties and constitutional protections.

These examples illustrate how the politically connected are allowed to escape responsibility for their conduct. Conversely, those viewed as opponents of the government and average citizens are held to account for their actions. A legal system that prosecutes citizens differently based on an individual's connections to the political powers in government, is a system that will not last.

Without an independent Congress, there is no power to check an abusive executive or even a dictator.

Political parties do not want members of Congress to serve as fiduciaries to the institution of Congress. They want their members of Congress to be loyal only to them. As such, political parties can be used to establish tyranny.

The House of Representatives can always impeach a president that acts illegally; however, removing the president is unlikely since it requires a two-thirds vote of the Senate. Unless the president's party acts based on the evidence, not a desire for political protection, the president remains in office, no matter the criminality of the conduct. Since the president controls the federal government's entire legal apparatus for investigating, charging for crimes, or otherwise bringing suit against the illegal activities of federal officials or the government, there are no effective legal means to hold anyone in the federal government accountable for its crimes.

Certainly, citizens can speak out, protest, demonstrate, sometimes complain at government meetings, or send nasty letters to our elected officials. Ultimately, however, they will be ignored if the government wants to ignore them. Or they are arrested if the government wants them arrested, as illustrated by the abusive treatment of parents seeking answers from the Loudoun County School Board that covered up the actions of male sexual predators assaulting female students in female bathrooms.

Citizens could emulate the peaceful resistance or nationwide strikes that Mahatma Gandhi led in India. Unfortunately, if peaceful resistance is undertaken, it is likely the federal government will use the tactics of the British Empire and brutally attack objectionable citizens, or worse. A recent incident supports this proposition. In a small Pennsylvania town, twenty heavily armed FBI agents, with weapons drawn, supported by a fleet of armored vehicles, arrested a pro-life activist at his home while he was playing with his seven children in the front yard. The FBI does not disclose the crime, but press reports suggest he was arrested for pushing a man who was verbally harassing one of his young children. State authorities refused to prosecute the alleged "crime." The person being pushed filed a criminal complaint in state court but failed to show at trial, so the case was dismissed. The FBI, however, targets certain groups, like pro-life advocates and parents who speak out at school board meetings. It dubs them domestic terrorists, yet leftist radicals who burn down cities are seldom prosecuted.

The only power "We the people" have is our vote for Congress.

Citizens do not vote for the president; that is done by the electoral college and a convoluted quilt of state voting laws, state Secretaries of State, and judicial proceedings. The justices of the Supreme Court and the judges on the lower courts are appointed, as are the millions of nameless bureaucrats that make laws daily by regulating almost every aspect of society.

Our right to vote for members of Congress is extraordinarily powerful. It is a legal mechanism that provides for a peaceful revolution. Citizens can vote out the entire House of Representatives every two years; the entire Senate over six years and elect a Congress whose members function as trustees of the Constitution and fiduciaries that ensure Congress is a check on the powers of the president and the judiciary. Only by electing such a Congress can we ensure our Constitution will protect us.

CHAPTER 7

Second Horseman, Unjust Laws

The massive national debt imposes unjust laws on our children.

"Blessed are the young, for they shall inherit the National Debt." Why would Herbert Hoover, the man many blame for the Great Depression, make such a comment? There is a simple answer. If the federal government taxed current citizens the total amount of the programs it funds, there would be a tax revolt against what citizens consider "unjust laws."

Our elected representatives avoid accountability and confrontation by shifting the cost of today's bloated government to future generations who have no say in the accumulated debt. Each dollar borrowed today is a dollar our posterity will have to repay for what we have spent, and with interest.

The United States is 247 years old. By the end of Biden's term in office, the last seven of forty-six presidents, in their forty-four combined years in office, will have borrowed $34 trillion, in addition to the trillions in annual appropriations, to run the nation. That is 94% of the estimated FY 2025 national debt of $36 trillion. Each taxpayer's share of the national debt exceeds $250,000. The average personal income in the U.S. is $63,211. The Congressional Budget Office estimates that our national debt will increase to 181% of our GDP in 2053. Over the next ten years, the federal government will pay an additional $10.5 trillion in interest on the debt.

Thomas Jefferson warned us that the public debt is the greatest danger to be feared. To preserve our independence, we must not let our rulers load us with perpetual debt. How can this happen under a constitution establishing a Republic of limited governmental power and a Bill of Rights to protect individuals and their property?

Unfortunately, our Constitution is only as good as the people who manage the nation. It has few guardrails as to the type of government it can legally establish. As such, it can function as an unrestrained capitalist economy, a highly regulated market, socialist, or mixed economy, as long as our officials are elected and give lip service to the Constitution. This debate plays out daily in Washington as Conservatives, Progressives and moderates advocate for dramatically different forms of government. The only issue both parties have historically agreed upon is to spend more money.

Moreover, a sober reading of the words of our Constitution illuminates the fact that Article I, sec. 8 of the Constitution establishes the federal government as an unrestrained tax master that has unlimited taxing, spending, and borrowing authority. Subsequently, the Sixteenth Amendment to the Constitution expanded Congress' power to tax without apportioning taxes among the states. Its power to tax extends to all gross income and is freely used to reward friends with subsidies, deductions, and tax credits to minimize the taxes of those that support the ruling government's policies. While the marginal tax rates were above 90% from 1944 to 1963, those rates were substantially lowered by Presidents Reagan, Bush, and Trump as the tax code was loaded with gifts to private industries, from semiconductors to NASCAR and horse racing, and low carried-interest tax rates for the wealthiest.

Federal taxing power solidly rests on U.S. Supreme Court decisions that hold high taxes are not considered involuntary servitude or the taking of property. Excessive, even confiscatory taxes, are authorized under the Constitution. To the federal government, taxation is a means to collect money to run the government for its political purposes. It is up to the voters to determine the value they receive for their taxes.

The almost absolute powers of the federal government were recognized by the U.S. Supreme Court as early as 1819 in *McCulloch v. Maryland.* While the case involved the power of the state of Maryland to tax a national bank established by Congress, Chief Justice Marshall used the case to cement the scope of federal power. Marshall not only solidified all the federal government's enumerated powers; he also broadly applied the "necessary and proper clause" to establish broad implied and incidental federal powers. He indicated no phrase in the Constitution limits the use of these implied powers.

Marshall's holding shows that Congress has almost unlimited taxing power as long as it exercises it to "benefit the nation." In Marshall's view, anything limiting federal power would change the character of the Constitution. While Marshall recognized that taxing is the power to destroy, he justified its use by noting it is given to officials elected by the voters. He acknowledged that abuse of federal power would create a loss of confidence in government. His remedy for abuse is tautological; it is found in the structure of the government itself.

Democrats and Republicans are jointly responsible for the national debt. Republicans, for all their righteous calls for fiscal restraint, are responsible for 57% of it through FY 2022. This percentage, however, will come into balance as the Biden administration is projected to add another $6 trillion or more to the national debt by the end of its first term.

The chart on the next page illustrates that both parties equally share the blame for the national debt.

Natl Debt increases		Republican	Democrat	Total National Debt
H. Hoover	FY 1930-1933	+$5.7 billion		$23 billion
F. Roosevelt	FY 1934-1945		+$236 billion	$259 billion
H. Truman	FY 1946-1953		+$7.3 billion	$266 billion
D. Eisenhower	FY 1954-1961	+$23 billion		$289 billion
J. Kennedy	FY 1962-1964		+$22.8 billion	$312 billion
L.B. Johnson	FY 1965-1969		+$41.8 billion	$353 billion
R. Nixon	FY 1970-1974	+$121.1 billion		$475 billion
G. Ford	FY 1975-1977	+$223.7 billion		$698 billion
J. Carter	FY 1978-1981		+$299 billion	$997 billion

R. Reagan	FY 1982-1989	+$1.86 trillion		$2.857 trillion
G.H.W. Bush	FY 1990-1993	+$1.55 trillion		$4.407 trillion
W. J. Clinton	FY 1994-2001		+$1.4 trillion	$5.807 trillion
G.W. Bush	FY 2002-2009	+$5.85 trillion		$11.665 trillion
B. Obama	FY 2010-2017		+$8.6 trillion	$20.257 trillion
D. Trump	FY 2018-2021	+$8.2 trillion		$28.845 trillion
J. Biden (estimate)	FY 2022-2025		+ $7.2 trillion	$36.00 trillion
Party totals		**$17.83 trillion**	**$17.82 trillion**	

Since all branches of the federal government have manipulated the Constitution to acquire unlimited federal power to tax, spend, and borrow, how can citizens control it?

There is a passage in Martin Luther King, Jr's *Letter from Birmingham Jail* on unjust laws that should be mandatory reading for every lawmaker. It extends far beyond the heinous evils and unjust nature of racial discrimination. It is a timeless analysis of the fundamental attributes of structuring "just laws" in a democracy.

King is asked: "How can you advocate breaking some laws and obeying others?" He replied, "...there are two types of laws: there are just laws, and there are unjust laws." He explained the moral basis for the distinction. But his two examples of the differences provide insight into structuring "just laws" in a democracy.

To Dr. King, an unjust law is a law the majority imposes on a minority but not itself. A just law applies to all equally.

Secondly, an unjust law is inflicted upon a group that had no part in its passing, e.g., those deprived of the right to vote.

While these principles apply to racial discrimination, they can also be applied to the rapidly increasing, massive national debt. Future generations, who have not been given a "say" or "vote" in the spending process, or electing those who make the decisions to spend, will be required to repay our debt for benefits we received today. Future generations are being told, "Pay our bills."

It is improbable the federal government and today's citizens will pay off this debt in their lifetimes. We are living on the future productivity of those who have not voted for the debt being created.

Other than the writings of Dr. King and a few leaders of peaceful resistance movements, the discussion of "unjust laws" is a subject left to philosophers and ethicists. The immenseness of the national debt and its impact on future generations requires debate today, especially by federal officeholders and candidates. We can no longer separate questions of morality from the consequences of legislative and executive actions like thoughtless increases in the debt ceiling and new open-ended programs.

We can easily claim there is nothing we can do; our

elected leaders control the budget, spending, and continuing increases in the debt ceiling. Moreover, we are constantly told those borrowed funds go to the many "good causes" supporters claim must be addressed.

Notwithstanding the immense power exercised by federal officials, citizens are responsible for the actions of the state. If we continue to allow the federal government to amass debt, we are telling future generations "They have no rights. They are servants of the federal government." At this point, the U.S. becomes an unjust nation to its children.

CHAPTER 8

Third Horseman, Control

Federal climate change policy is not about protecting the environment. It is about control over society. The apocalyptic talk about climate change is nothing more than a diversionary tactic used by the Climate Fear Industry ("CFI"), a coalition of the federal government, the Progressive Left, and its mainstream propaganda press, to justify the repressive actions of the federal government and the enrichment of its supporters in the green industry. The many unworkable laws promoting a green economy and the trillions in federal appropriations and tax credits to address climate change will not, as President Obama promised, slow the "rise of the oceans or heal the planet."

The CFI has the world obsessing over whether the planet has 10, 20, or 50 years before the eve of destruction. The CFI, however, is nothing more than a coordinated effort by the green industry and its well-funded advocacy groups to lobby for legislation that benefits them. Open Secrets reports the business community spent $4.1 billion in 2022 to lobby

Congress and the administration on the many issues business has before government. What is not disclosed in that report is the CFI industry spent $4.5 billion in 2021 to lobby Congress and the administration to eliminate fossil fuels and nuclear energy. These CFIs represent themselves as being for the public good, not lobbyists. Critics have labeled CFI as "The Anti-Industry Industry." The top 25 CFI groups spent more than four times what the fossil fuel and nuclear energy groups spent and more than the entire business community spent on all of its lobbying.

The goal of CFI is not to protect the climate; its goal is to control society while generating money, and lots of it, for its supporters. A recent Morgan Stanley report finds that to achieve net-zero carbon emissions will require the world to spend $50 trillion, in the next three decades, on the green technologies, including on-shore and off-shore wind, solar, electric vehicles, carbon capture and storage, hydrogen, and biofuels.

Government's efforts to control society and CFI efforts to enrich its benefactors will have little impact on stopping climate change. A recent Manhattan Institute report concludes green technologies "cannot be surged in times of need, are not inherently clean nor even independent of hydrocarbons, and are not cheap." The study points out the hard realities that the world runs on hydrocarbons, which are in almost every product, machine, and electronic device. The report makes clear that even a digital society needs fossil fuels to ensure its green technologies can operate. "[D]igital devices and hardware… require, on average, about 1000 times more energy to fabricate, pound for pound, than the products that dominated the 20th century."

The study compares energy use in various industries. Its findings are startling. "Thus, the global fabrication of smartphones now uses 15% as much energy as does the entire automotive industry, even though a car weights 10,000 times more than a smartphone."

Its most sobering conclusions are that a zero-energy transition path would require a greater expansion of "all global energy infrastructures [than has] taken place over the past 60 years." Moreover, the minerals needed for the green technology transition "require a quantity of minerals that exceeds the known global reserves of those minerals."

The only certainty of pushing a net-zero energy transition is the government will gain more control over citizens and industrial production and the CFI groups will become fabulously wealthy. Those transitions have already started.

The CFI is the grand master of imposing regulations to control society.

Citizens of the United States already live under a legal framework that contains over 3,000 separate criminal offenses in 50 titles of the U.S. Code, 23,000 pages of federal law, over 200,000 regulations, and frequent Executive Orders that limit actions deemed objectionable to the kakistocracy. Many of these laws and regulations are environmental. Additionally, the president has in reserve 135 emergency powers allowing it to assume control over industrial production, communications, banking, and most aspects of commerce. Most of these emergency laws are effective when the president declares them effective.

The size of government and the laws it enacts determine the amount of freedom Americans exercise. The CFI is successfully establishing a massive federal government that centralizes power around its agenda.

The CFI plays the federal regulatory system like a grand master pianist. By incorporating Citizen Suit provisions in all environmental laws, the federal government allows the CFI to block many of the permits needed to enhance energy supplies or construct almost anything.

The CFI also demands the federal government break up banks if they make loans or investments to fossil fuel companies or operations that they assert harm the earth.

Restricting fossil fuels will directly lead to the demise of the United States.

The most egregious part of the federal climate policy is its attempt to reduce and eventually eliminate fossil fuels, the foundation for civilization's progress and wealth. Fossil fuels can be consumed for energy, but they are also the building blocks of almost everything society makes and uses. Green energy, however, can only be consumed. It cannot be incorporated into another product. Moreover, fossil fuels represent 84% of all energy, while green energy is around 5%. A rapid transition to all-green energy is impossible. Fossil fuels make too many products, help grow the food supply, heat too many homes, and power too many cars to be eliminated without causing a collapse of the country. Compounding the problem is that the federal government has placed restrictions on the use of its energy reserves, which is forcing it to rely on a few authoritarian countries for the fossil fuels needed to run society.

If the CFI successfully eliminates fossil fuels, over 6,000 products that citizens use daily will also be eliminated.

Ranken Energy Corporation presented a sampling of the at-risk products:

Air mattresses, Ammonia, Antifreeze, Antihistamines, Antiseptics, Artificial limbs, Artificial turf, Asphalt, Aspirin, Awnings, Backpacks, Balloons, Ballpoint pens, Bandages, Beach umbrellas, Boats, Cameras, Candies and gum, Candles, Car battery cases, Car enamel, Cassettes, Caulking, CDs/computer disks, Cell phones, Clothes, Clothesline, Clothing, Coffee makers, Cold cream, Combs, Computer keyboards, Computer monitors, Cortisone, Crayons, Credit cards, Curtains, Dashboards, Denture adhesives, Dentures, Deodorant, Detergent, Dice, Dishwashing liquid, Dog collars, Drinking cups, Dyes, Electric blankets, Electrical tape, Enamel, Epoxy paint, Eyeglasses, Fan belts, Faucet washers, Fertilizers, Fishing boots, Fishing lures, Floor wax, Food preservatives, Footballs, Fuel tanks, Glue, Glycerin, Golf bags, Golf balls, Guitar strings, Hair coloring, Hair curlers, Hand lotion, Hearing aids, Heart valves, House paint, Hula hoops, Ice buckets, Ice chests, Ice cube trays, Ink, Insect repellent, Insecticides, Insulation, iPad/iPhone, Kayaks, Laptops, Life jackets, Light-weight aircraft, Lipstick, Loudspeakers, Lubricants, Luggage, Model cars, Mops, Motorcycle helmets, Movie film, Nail polish, Noise insulation, Nylon rope, Oil filters, Packaging, Paint brushes, Paint roller, Pajamas, Panty hose, Parachutes, Perfumes, Permanent press, Petroleum jelly, Pharmaceuticals, Pillow filling, Plastic toys, Plastics, Plywood adhesive, Propane, Purses, Putty, Refrigerants, Refrigerator linings, Roller skate wheels, Roofing, Rubber cement, Rubbing alcohol, Safety glasses, Shampoo, Shaving cream, Shoe polish, Shoes/sandals, Shower curtains, Skateboards, Skis Soap dishes, Soft contact lenses, Solar panels, Solvents, Spacesuits, Sports car bodies, Sunglasses, Surf boards, Swimming pools Synthetic rubber Telephones Tennis rackets Tents Tires Tool boxes Tool racks, Toothbrushes, Toothpaste, Transparent tape, Trash bags, Truck and automobile parts, Tubing, TV cabinets, Umbrellas, Unbreakable dishes, Upholstery, Vaporizers, Vinyl flooring, Vitamin capsules, Water pipes, Wind turbine blades, Yarn.

Product and appliance restrictions.

The federal government regulates almost every item in the home, including dishwashers, washing machines, showerheads, toilets, ceiling fans, light bulbs, heating and air conditioning units, water heaters, freezers, stoves, ovens, refrigerators, and conventional cooking products. Seventy-five regulatory standards cover these products. The Consumer Product Safety Commission regulates another 15,000 products, from coffee pots to ink cartridges.

Food and the packaging to preserve it are next.

The CFI wants to ban many common foods, including sugar, chocolate, coffee, meat, palm oil, soybeans, mineral water, plastic bottles, fish, salmon, rice and cereal, and fruits and vegetables that require water.

The CFI identifies the top 10 foods that harm the climate: lamb, beef, pork, chicken, turkey, salmon, canned tuna, cheese, eggs, and potatoes. Once the foods are identified, the regulations to reduce or eliminate them begin.

The radical Left also has 25 reasons for banning plastic packaging that preserves our food.

Restrictions on housing.

In addition to regulating everyday products, the CFI is now proposing Americans live in urban settlements. The Climate and Community Project at the University of California, Davis, issued a study describing how to achieve nirvana. It proposes reducing the use of cars, even in the suburbs, by forcing high-density urban living on all people. Transportation would be bicycling, walking, and building mass transportation everywhere. Almost everyone would live in a small apartment in a "livable neighborhood." This plan would force the displacement of millions of rural Americans. Let's call this "brilliant" idea "The Great Resettlement," a softer label than a "21c. Trail of Tears." The concept underlying this report has been incorporated into Biden's failed infrastructure proposal. Biden's budget proposes $10 billion for grants to local communities that change zoning laws to limit single-family homes.

Trillions in subsidies for clean energy cannot be effectively utilized.

While the federal government is *de facto* mandating an all-electric transportation system, it ignores a few basic facts. Due to massive government subsidies, automakers produce more electric vehicles ("EVs") than existing charging stations can charge. The situation will get worse as projections have EV sales increasing to 30% of auto sales by 2030. Auto production is estimated to increase from 500,000 EVs sold today to 4.7 million in 2030. Moreover, each EV has a battery pack containing 2,000 plus lithium-ion cells that must be charged. The U.S. will need 20-50% more electricity to charge all these batteries. Cars will be competing with homes and businesses for electricity. This competition will make electricity much more expensive. The inability to supply affordable electricity is why the CFI proposes to order citizens to live in small apartments close to food supplies and work. California is giving us a glimpse of the future. The state ordered residents not to charge their electric vehicles in heat waves due to insufficient electricity.

Windmills also have problems. With the massive subsidies available to the business community, the U.S. is building more windmills than can be hooked to the grid. The U.S. has an installed capacity of 1,250 gigawatts of power, and there are currently 2,020 gigawatts of energy capacity waiting to be connected. Wait times can be years, and very costly to integrate with the grid once capacity increases. Moreover, when the wind stops blowing, backup energy must be supplied. The current backup energy is fossil fuels since they are reliable and plentiful. Without fossil fuels, the only backup is a few hours of battery storage. David Wojick, an expert in the interrelations of science, technology, and policy, concludes, "It is simply impossible to provide enough energy storage [without fossil fuels] to make renewables reliable."

Additionally, wind farm output can drop below 10% of its rated capacity for days, and solar power disappears at night and drops below 50% capacity on cloudy days. Green technology capacity determinations are meaningless. They are too reliant on the weather. Green technology cannot function without fossil fuel backup energy. Compounding the difficulties, when the wind blows hard and the sun shines bright, green technology generates more energy than can be used. Since the grid cannot handle the excess, it must be dumped, which can be very costly.

As if the above does not raise enough serious concerns over the viability of green technology, the Wall Street Journal cited a report by the International Energy Agency that estimated to achieve the environmentalists' zero-emissions goal will require the construction of 49.7 million miles of transmission lines. That is enough lines to wrap around the world 2,000 times and this infrastructure would need to be in place by 2040.

Green energy will turn the U.S. into a hazardous waste dump.

From the Industrial Revolution to the 1970s, the federal government and American industry ignored the hazardous waste generated by industry and the military. The waste was dumped in the "back 40" or local rivers, pits, ponds, lagoons, and thousands of backyards. In the mid-1970s, when the Congress recognized the massive hazardous waste problem, it enacted the Resource Conservation and Recovery Act ("RCRA") to clean up the hazardous waste. RCRA was a cradle-to-grave strict liability approach that was costly and time-consuming but effective. By the end of the 1990s, the nation was cleansed of improperly disposed of hazardous waste.

Unfortunately, the federal government has forgotten the environmental problems and costs caused by the improper management of hazardous waste. To avoid future waste management issues, Congress should be proactive by educating the green industry on the many waste streams generated by its technology before it generates any waste. Once the green technology industry understands its waste streams, it can begin to understand the real cost of its business.

Solar Panels.

78 million tons of panels will reach the end of their useful life between now and 2050. Solar is only 2.3% of our electric generation; extrapolating to 50% of electric generation by 2050 would mean almost 2 billion tons of solar panel waste would be in need of disposal between now and 2050. There is currently little recycling of solar panels due to the low value of the materials and the high recycling cost. Moreover, landfilling may not be possible since solar panels contain silver, copper, cadmium, and lead, i.e., hazardous wastes, making disposal enormously more expensive than disposing of solid waste. Average landfill costs are $54 per ton for solid waste. Hazardous waste, however, is priced by the pound. Depending on how much of the waste is hazardous and whether it can be separated from the non-hazardous parts, the cost of disposing hundreds of billion pounds of hazardous waste could be in the hundreds of billions, or trillions of dollars or more depending on regulatory requirements.

Wind Turbines.

An estimated 720,000 blades, 100 to 300 feet long, will require disposal over the next 20 years. They are too large for solid waste landfills, and transportation costs are high. The estimated cost to decommission each wind tower is around $532,000. Another study, however, estimates the cost at four times that amount. Wind capacity is anticipated to double by 2030 and quadruple by 2050.

A study published in Environmental Research and Letters by two Harvard researchers, found "that the transition to wind or solar power in the United States would require five to 20 times more land area than previously thought, and if such large-scale wind farms were built, would warm average surface temperatures over the continental U.S. by 0.24 degrees Celsius." The same study found "If your perspective is the next 10 years, wind power actually has-in some respects-more climate impact than coal or gas. If your perspective is the next thousand years, then wind power has enormously less climate impact than coal or gas."

Cost estimates to build a green U.S. range from $2.7 trillion to $93 trillion. Serious experts, however, believe costs are only calculable with specific policy proposals. Since these costs are far in the future, it is unlikely the private sector companies building the turbines using federal tax credits and grants are incorporating disposal costs into the price of the turbine. If the private sector companies do not establish large reserve funds to cover the future costs of disposal or recycling, it is likely the cost will be forced onto society if the companies go bankrupt. Since the objective of RCRA is to prevent this type of problem, Congress should thoroughly analyze the waste issues from green energy before giving trillions to the private sector to create an avoidable and massively expensive hazardous waste problem.

Electric vehicles.

The U.S. Energy Information Agency ("EIA") projects there will be 672 million EVs in the U.S. by 2050 and 2.21 billion worldwide. According to Autoweek, the battery pack on the new GMC Hummer EV weighs in at 2,923 pounds, more than the weight of a Honda Civic.

What to do with the millions of EV batteries at the end of their useful life is controversial. Historically, battery recycling operations have not been the best stewards of the environment. Many of these facilities have been designated Superfund (contaminated waste) sites in need of costly cleanup. Tesla, however, recycles all of its batteries at no cost to consumers. Tesla pays recyclers $4.50 per pound to recycle the battery packs, or $6,750 per car. At this time the other automakers are not recycling the batteries installed in their cars.

The cost to recycle hundreds of millions of EV batteries will be in the hundreds of billions of dollars, perhaps in the trillions. Currently there are huge federal subsidies, in the form of tax credits, to build EV battery recycling plants under the IRA. The larger issue however, is who pays for the recycling or disposal of EV batteries when the battery recyclers go out of business or the federal government runs out of money, or has budget cuts? Who is responsible for paying for the batteries at the end of their life, the car owner or the auto maker? It's a long-term problem that cannot be avoided in light of a long history of poor waste management by the recycling industry.

The U.S. does not have the materials to transition to a green society.

The hazardous materials used to make EV batteries are mined worldwide. While China controls the supply chain for these materials, the minerals come from DR Congo (cobalt), Mexico, Chile, and Australia (lithium), Indonesia, China, and Russia (nickel), and South Africa, China, Australia, and Mexico (manganese)—primarily repressive countries with few environmental protections.

In our age of "social justice," the U.S federal government and American industry ignore the harms caused by the overseas mining operations, including the use slave or child labor. Moreover, the residual mining waste is left untreated in developing countries to contaminate local land, water and harm the health of its citizens. All these harms are done to people throughout the world so that our federal government can implement its green agenda.

The sun is beginning to set on the U.S.

As the CFI aggressively promotes its climate change agenda, the federal government is waist-deep in debt and international conflicts from its chaotic Afghanistan surrender, potential war with China over Taiwan, the Ukraine conflict with Russia, and the nuclearization of Iran and North Korea and most recently, the Israel-Hamas conflict. In the middle of these international conflicts, the federal government drained its Strategic Petroleum Reserve to lower gasoline prices before the 2022 election. It has sent a large part of its weapons stockpile to Ukraine. A distracted U.S. military system missed a Chinese spy balloon that was so visible that citizens on the ground in Montana noticed it and brought it to the attention of the U.S military. While the world views the U.S. as weak and unfocused, our generals focus on training our military to be social justice warriors.

The green obsession of the federal government will result in a transition from affordable and available energy for the nation to intermittent energy for use in homes, offices, industry, and charging electric vehicles. Its green policies will likely result in food shortages, a lack of manufacturing, and the design of less effective appliances by bureaucrats. Moreover, without fossil fuels, many of the needed products consumers use to make everyday life easier will simply disappear. This dreary green society will be waist deep in hazardous waste from the spent green technologies.

As mentioned in Chapter 2, China confronted an existential situation in 1433. Fearing its political opponents, it destroyed the activity that brought the nation its wealth - its ocean-going fleet. That decision started China's decent into poverty for almost 500 years. Bright lights are flashing caution to the U.S. It's on a path with its green obsession that is likely to destroy the country by driving it into poverty by restricting energy, food, and innovation.

The federal government is so preoccupied with its continuous political manipulation that it cannot discern the state of the nation. The federal government is managing so many activities that it has created a government that is too big and far too complex to govern the nation. To rescue itself and to save the nation, it must devolve many of its domestic responsibilities to the states so it can focus on the defense of the nation and maintaining a strong economy.

If the federal government is unable to devolve some of its domestic powers to the states so they can help manage the country, the United States will become a failed state.

CHAPTER 9

Fourth Horseman, Secrecy

Since the Deep State is a secret group, it is unknown if it exists. Yet belief in its existence persists as a means of explaining the bizarre actions of a secretive federal government. The Deep State is believed to be a group of influential members of the government, military, finance, and defense industries that secretly undertake illegal activities in the political interest of the country's ruling elite. Starting with the deceit concerning the Central Intelligence Agency's ("CIA") orchestrated coup in Iran and Guatemala in the 1950s, the years of lies concerning the need for the Viet Nam War, and the Senate's 1975 Church Committee Report finding evidence of the CIA and FBI's illegal secret spying on the American people, there is an increasing belief that someone, likely a secret group, is running the United States other than its elected officials.

In the last decade, the federal government's activities have become more secretive and bizarre. Who in the DOJ/FBI allowed the Russian collusion story to continue against a sitting president, while knowing it was false and seriously undermining the ability of a sitting president to run the country? Who in the FBI withheld from the American public, for many years, the story of the Biden Syndicate's history of international bribery, extortion, and money laundering? Who allowed the DOJ to knowingly file false affidavits with the FISA Court so federal agencies could spy on and indict Trump campaign staff members?

There are too many questions about the illegal activities of a few federal agencies. The many intelligence and law enforcement agencies have, for decades, intentionally refused to provide Congress with the information needed for oversight of their many seemingly-illegal activities. The eight most disingenuous words federal investigative agencies use to hide their criminal activity are "I can't answer, the matter is under investigation." These words are used to obstruct, mislead, and delay congressional investigations into the legality of many executive branch activities. These words destroy the principle of Separation of Powers by placing certain executive branch agencies above the law. The intelligence and investigative agencies have made themselves exempt from congressional oversight. These eight words allow the federal government the secrecy it needs to operate, investigate, persecute, prosecute, and terrorize citizens it finds objectionable.

What can be done?

For the last several years evidence was uncovered that points to a Deep State bureaucracy that actively works to deceive those with authority to investigate it.

During the 2020 campaign, fifty-one former intelligence

officials, in support of President Biden's election efforts, signed an open letter, organized by Antony Blinken, now Secretary of State under Biden, that falsely stated the information released by the New York Post concerning the contents of Hunter Biden's laptop, had "all the classic earmarks" of Russian disinformation. The contents of the laptop provided evidence of payments to Hunter Biden by the Burisma Oil Company for access to the then-vice president of the United States, Joe Biden. Biden used the letter in a candidate's debate to shut down all discussion of his role in suspected bribery and money laundering. The actions of the former intelligence officials resulted in direct interference in a federal election to control who rules the nation. Biden won in 2020, and Trump lost. Polls show that 16% of Biden voters would have voted differently had they known the Hunter Biden laptop information was authentic. Now almost all the mainstream media agree the laptop is genuine.

A question worth pondering is why President Trump's DOJ/FBI decided not to investigate the laptop? Was the DOJ/FBI coordinating with Biden's campaign against Trump, believing Trump might be a potential disruptor of the Deep State? Or was Trump intimidated by the Deep State? Trump's actions make no sense in light of him seeking reelection.

Another example comes from the 2024 presidential campaign of Robert F. Kennedy, Jr. He emphatically states there is evidence that the CIA killed his uncle, president John F. Kennedy ("JFK"). It's been sixty years since the assassination of JFK. President after president have refused to release the crucial 5,000 pages of the investigation.

During the 2016 campaign, Trump promised to release the records. He got elected and refused to release the records. In the 2020 campaign, Biden promised to release the remaining records. Once elected, Biden refused to honor his campaign promise. The refusal to release the records only heightens the speculation that the CIA assassinated JFK, and continues its control over individuals occupying the office of the president.

Then there is all the DOJ/FBI corruption set out in the *Horowitz* and *Durham* reports, all of which has gone unpunished.

Unfortunately, since the administration of Richard M. Nixon presidents have asserted Executive Privilege thirty times to block congressional investigations. Presidential assertions included protecting a president's brother (Billy Carter), girlfriend (Monica Lewinsky), mismanagement of federal funds (Solyndra), foreign affairs debacles (Hillary Clinton/Benghazi), U.S. sanctioned gun running (Attorney General Holder/Fast and Furious), and the Watergate tapes. By forcing Congress to issue subpoenas to secure requested documents, presidents achieve their goal of protecting corruption by forcing Congress into years of legal battles to obtain non-privileged documents. Moreover, Congress is forced to negotiate over its document request and usually only receives a small portion of its request.

Finding and eliminating corruption is for the benefit of the nation. Hiding corruption does not assist the president in the faithful execution of the law. The DOJ/FBI/CIA's long-running minuet of never sharing information with congressional committees is a mechanism of deceit, not of protecting the independence and effectiveness of law enforcement, the identities of informants, avoiding pre-trial publicity, or interfering with prosecutorial discretion. The Supreme Court has long recognized the implied power of Congress to investigate and to compel the production of information from the executive branch The DOJ/FBI/CIA continuously refuse to comply with the Constitution. This resistance should tell the American people all they need to know.

Executive Privilege is not found in the Constitution. While the courts recognize a limited use of it, the basis for it is found in the opinions of the DOJ. Its parameters are not clear. To the extent Executive Privilege exists, it is limited to the quintessential powers of the president that cannot be delegated away. It should only be asserted to preserve core constitutional duties such as presidential communications, deliberations, and national security. Claiming it beyond the core constitutional functions is a delaying tactic that often allows illegal conduct to continue.

As to documents related to alleged criminal activity in the executive branch, no president should ever be intentionally or unintentionally covering it up. The American Bar Association writes, "Under the U.S. Constitution, the president as commander in chief is given broad powers to classify and declassify such information, often through Executive Orders." While there are procedures for declassifying the materials, a president, except for certain materials such as nuclear secrets, has almost total control to declassify records by Executive Order. Presidents at all times have the power to put sunlight on government corruption. When they choose not to expose corruption, it is an intentional coverup.

If a president truly wants to root out government corruption, he should issue an Executive Order waiving Executive Privilege and provide all documents sought by congressional investigators relating to the criminal activities of federal agencies and personnel, including classified documents. A few very relevant, long-standing, unanswered, congressional requests of the DOJ/FBI/CIA that must be responded to include: investigative materials on the Durham, Mueller, and Inspector General Horowitz Reports, payments received by Joe and Hunter Biden from foreign countries and the many related Suspicious Activity Reports, all matters associated with the development of a two-tier system of justice, efforts by the federal government to force private sector social media companies to manipulate information distributed to the public, and all other matters of high-level agency corruption. Moreover, the president should release the remaining documents of the Warren Commission's Report on the assassination of JFK.

By taking this approach, the president will tremendously assist the congressional investigations focused on the misconduct of the federal investigative agencies. Moreover, it frees the president from any conflict of interest he might have by investigating departments he leads.

Suppose executive branch personnel refuse to testify or take the Fifth by asserting their constitutional rights not to be a witness against themselves. In that case, Congress can grant Use Immunity, which compels their testimony by providing immunity to the witness for the new information provided. A witness that refuses to testify after being given Use Immunity can be cited for contempt of Congress and imprisoned.

It's time a president of the U.S. gets serious about corruption in government. More intriguing would be if a president followed this advice. The nation might discover if someone other than the president is running the federal government.

PART III

Before Devolving Power to the States, Congress Must Clean Up the Mess It Created

CHAPTER 10

If It's Constitutional to Increase Federal Power, It's Constitutional to Decrease Federal Power

The growth of the federal government has been the only unifying ambition of Congress, presidents, and the courts since the dawn of the Republic. It was accomplished by its many legal and illegal undertakings: wars, territorial acquisitions, the conquering indigenous people, Manifest Destiny, the Civil War Amendments that placed the federal government as "protector" of the people and supervisor of states, the expansionary social programs enacted during the Great Depression, the Civil Rights and Environmental movements of the 1960s and 1970s, and the massive increases in the national debt from Ronald Reagan to Joe Biden.

The constitutional foundation for expanding federal power, however, starts with Chief Justice Marshall's 1819 decision in *McCulloch v. Maryland*. As noted in Chapter 7, "Marshall not only solidified all the federal government's enumerated powers, he also broadly applied the 'necessary

and proper clause' to establish broad implied and incidental
federal powers. He indicated no phrase in the Constitution
limits the use of these implied powers."

As the first significant decision on the scope of federal
power, Marshall used several provisions of the Constitution
to expand the power of the federal government and limit the
power of the states. In subsequent cases, he continued to
expand federal power by holding Congress has the power to
regulate interstate commerce by regulating monopolies. By
using undefined terms, Marshall granted Congress the
authority to make all laws which are necessary and proper
for carrying out its lawmaking powers. His decisions
elevated the Supreme Court to being the final arbiter of
constitutional issues as well as issues that could be
considered somewhat related to federal power. He achieved
this result by skillfully combining the Constitution's
enumerated powers with its implied powers. By doing so,
national power could be exercised by the federal government
in an almost unlimited manner.

By ignoring, however, that the federal government only
exists by the consent of the people, Marshall designed a
power structure that contained few limits on how the people
could restrain a corrupt government short of a revolution.
While he recognized the abuse of power by the officials
would cause a loss of confidence in government, the only
remedy he offered citizens was to rely on the structure of the
Constitution that grants citizens the power to elect officials.

While Marshall notes it is the structure of the Constitution
that protects the nation since federal officials are elected, he
fails to explain how the separation of powers structure of the
Constitution is essential to controlling federal power. Not

only must each branch of the federal government constantly check the power of the other branches, but every official must give absolute loyalty to the branch in which they serve to ensure the power of government is always limited to the powers granted by the Constitution. The official's loyalty to the branch of government it serves is its fiduciary duty. Moreover, it is the only mechanism by which these officials can be trustees of the Constitution.

Unfortunately, when the structure of the Constitution has been corrupted by elected officials who give loyalty to the political party that helped elect them rather than the institution in which they serve, the nation is run by politics, not the Constitution. Raw political power created a massive federal government by diminishing the sovereignty of the states.

In *real politic* thought, states retain the constitutional right of self-governance until the feds diminish it.

While the Supreme Court has held that a state does not lose its distinct and individual existence or its right of self-government by being part of the Union, such a holding is a pure illusion. Our Founding Fathers believed the national government was one of limited powers, having only those powers expressly granted by the Constitution. Therefore, powers other than those enumerated in the Constitution rest with States or the people. The founders enshrined this belief in the Tenth Amendment to the Constitution, which reads, "The powers not delegated to the United States by the Constitution, nor prohibited by it to the States, are reserved to the States respectively, or to the people."

As long as the federal government remained small in size and authority, the states did not generally question its power.

As the federal government expanded its powers to implement massive new social programs, the limits of national power became controversial. When the Supreme Court directly confronted the limits of federal power, it rendered the Tenth Amendment irrelevant.

The demise of the Tenth Amendment arose when the Department of Labor sought to regulate local wages. States argued wage regulation was not an enumerated federal power in the Constitution. Therefore, such power rested with the states. Unfortunately for the states, a unanimous Supreme Court in *United States v Darby* (1941) stripped all meaning from the Tenth Amendment. The court held the Tenth Amendment was merely a "truism" since the substance needs to be determined by what powers are delegated to the federal government from any part of the Constitution. In *Darby*, the court held the federal government has the constitutional authority to regulate wages under the Commerce Clause.

In addition to *Darby*, the federal government used the national tragedy of the Great Depression to complete its power grab with the support of the Supreme Court. Initially, there was resistance from the Supreme Court to expand federal power; however, after Roosevelt threatened to pack the court with his political supporters, the court acceded to his demands by interpreting the Constitution's Commerce, Spending, Tax, and Welfare clauses very broadly to enhance federal rule.

The ever-expanding Commerce Clause.

Using its expansive interpretation of the Commerce Clause "to regulate Commerce with foreign nations, among the several states, and with the Indian tribes," the Supreme Court sanctioned the massive growth of what has become the Administrative State. It transformed a country that practiced federalism (a system of government in which two levels of government control the same territory) into a nation of federal rule. Congress has passed so many new federal laws, no one knows how many. The federal government can now reach almost every activity in the country with its 200,000 plus regulations that govern labor, environment, securities, banking, manufacturing, even children's toys, the treatment of animals, and thousands of other activities.

The Supreme Court did not strike down a single law expanding federal power between 1937 and 1995. In 1995, it finally struck down a congressional enactment involving gun possession in a schoolyard. The question was whether one gun sufficiently impacted commerce and whether the federal government could regulate it. The court found that possessing a single firearm did not substantially impact interstate commerce. The Supreme Court then struck down another case involving violence against women as being intrastate, not interstate, commerce. After minimally limiting federal power, the Supreme Court returned to rubber-stamping all future congressional enactments.

Any gaps in federal power over the states are quickly filled by bribing states to pursue federal priorities.

A Brookings study on state budgets noted "In 1900, states and localities raised $1.75 for every $1 of federal revenue. They performed all government activities except national defense, foreign relations, [federal] court proceedings, and postal services." While the federal government made grants to the states in this period, those grants generally subsidized existing state programs.

Beginning with the Great Depression and forward, Congress enacted many new social programs, some of which it did not have the constitutional authority to implement. The federal government was creative in overcoming its lack of constitutional authority. Congress merely raised taxes to generate sufficient funds under its enlarged tax and spending powers to provide grants to states to incentivize *them* to implement federal wishes. There were around 132 state grant programs in 1960. Today the number of state grant programs ranges between 1,000 to 1,300. These programs cost the federal government between $721 billion and $1.2 trillion annually. The federal government taxes the American public to pay for the grants it makes to states. It collects the taxes and returns a portion of the money collected to the states after deducting its commission.

According to the Bureau of Census, federal grants to states in FY 2020 represent 35.9% of state revenues. While states accept these grants, they come with federal strings attached. Compliance with many federal mandates often distorts state priorities by displacing local programs that may be more significant to the state's citizens than the federal programs. Receipt of federal funds can require states to provide matching funds, compliance with federal mandates, and increased personnel.

There are only a few superficial limits on federal power over states.

There are only two marginal limitations on the extent of federal power over states. First, the federal government cannot regulate purely local activity; however, even this restriction on federal power is questionable. While the Supreme Court holds states have the power to control local issues, the Court, however, upheld the power of Congress over the production of agricultural products grown for personal consumption during the Great Depression. It also upheld federal control over marijuana grown for personal medicinal use. The court reasoned these local actions have cumulative impacts on commerce; as such, they are subject to federal regulation. Under the courts' broad interpretation of commerce, almost all local activities can be viewed as having a cumulative effect on interstate commerce.

The second judicially established limitation on federal power: it cannot commandeer state personnel or resources for federal purposes. As noted, the federal government easily gets around this limitation by bribing states with tax dollars paid to Washington by the people of the respective states.

States are beginning to resist oppressive federal regulation.

If the Constitution is flexible enough to allow the federal government to expand its power over states without changing it, it is also flexible enough to reverse the federal power grab without constitutional changes. States have started efforts to reverse national power. More than a few states are now resisting the implementation of federal programs they believe violate state sovereignty or are not being fairly compensated for managing.

State frustration with implementing federal programs started with the conflict over sanctuary states and cities during the Trump administration. Over three-hundred states

and cities refused to enforce federal immigration laws
requiring the deportation of unauthorized immigrants, even
though they accepted federal grant monies for law
enforcement and other local activities associated with these
programs.

The federal-state conflict, however, is over more than
sanctuary cities. Twenty-three states and the District of
Columbia have legalized marijuana, notwithstanding it is
illegal under federal law. Moreover, since the federal
government cannot commandeer states to implement federal
law, any attempt to condition the receipt of federal monies
must be clear enough for the state to decide whether or not
to accept the funds. Further, federal control over conditions
in grants to state or local governments cannot be so coercive
that the circumstances amount to a "gun to the head"
situation. States have utilized these limitations to take
federal funds without complying with the imposed
conditions.

In addition to the outright refusal of states to implement
federal programs not of their liking, there are federal
programs, such as environmental regulations, that states
want to implement, but the federal grants only cover a
fraction of the cost of implementation. States implement
approximately 96% of federally delegated environmental
programs but only receive funding for approximately 28%
of the cost of implementation. At some point, states will
refuse to implement the unwanted federal mandates and
underfunded federal programs. Once confronted, the federal
government will be forced to either drop the disliked
mandates, put more funding in the programs, or allow the
states to run the programs as they wish, without federal

mandates.

Complicating the long-festering federal-state conflict is the issue of state grant inequality. Naturally, while every federal program is paid for with the tax dollars citizens send to Washington, not all states receive a dollar-for-dollar return on the money its citizens send to Washington. According to a study in The Atlantic, "Which States Are Givers, and Which States Are Takers," the amount of money given to the respective states varies dramatically. South Carolina receives $7.87 for every dollar its citizens send to Washington in taxes. Other states are not so lucky. Fourteen states receive less grant money than they send to the federal government in taxes. These states include Delaware, Minnesota, Illinois, Nebraska, Ohio, Kansas, New York, Colorado, Utah, New Jersey, Oklahoma, Wyoming, Massachusetts and California.

The Feds Might Also Pull the Funding Plug.

Complicating state dissatisfaction with the federal grant programs is the federal government's financial mess: a $34 trillion national debt and annual trillion-dollar budget deficits. The federal government may no longer have the financial ability to fund state programs. The combination of state resistance and a *de facto,* bankrupt federal government opens the door for a reversal of power.

According to a study by the Congressional Research Service, more than half of the federal grant money goes to Medicaid, and the rest to highways, environment, child nutrition, disaster relief, tenant rental assistance, education for the disadvantaged, children's health insurance, and urban mass transit, among other programs. These are local issues that have been federalized by the mandates contained in the federal grants.

The federal government's interest payments for FY 2022 were $475 billion. In February 2022, however, the CBO projected that net interest costs could total $640 billion in 2023 and soar to $1.4 trillion in 2033. The historically low-interest rates kept interest payments manageable between 2009 and 2019. The combination of increasing national debt and soaring interest payments on the debt will cause interest payments alone to exceed the total amount of all grants made to states. This deficiency means the federal government will need to find hundreds of billions of dollars annually to service the increased debt, or it will need to find other budget reductions, such as state program grants, to remain in the same financial position as today.

These federal-state tensions will accelerate the devolution of power.

The conflicting trends of states not wanting to implement specific federal programs and the federal government not having sufficient money to fully compensate the states for implementing its programs will start the debate over which programs should be administered and by whom. States will have to decide what programs they genuinely want to implement. The federal government will have to prioritize the programs it wants fully implemented by states.

States will have to balance the loss of federal funds against the savings they can capture by eliminating the implementation of unneeded or unwanted federal programs. Initially, it might seem that the loss of federal funds would substantially impact states. However, that may not be the case since many states supplement the implementation of unwanted federal programs with state funds to meet grant conditions.

The Supreme Court has been a strong supporter of the federal government encroaching on state policy. If Congress seeks to return government to a shared power relationship with states as a means of managing its massive national debt, it is very likely one or more of the Democratic run states like New York, California, or Illinois, which rely on federal largesse, will sue the federal government for the loss of funding. Since the Supreme Court cannot order Congress to spend money, Congress can easily shrink the federal government by reducing grants to states. In the final analysis, "We the People" elect government to manage the affairs of the nation for the benefit of its people. Creating a government closer to the people should be an issue supported by all branches of the federal government. If not, someone will have to figure out how to pay for the excessive federal spending.

CHAPTER 11

Cleanup Task One: Congress Must First Reclaim the Emergency and War Powers Delegated to the President

By delegating significant emergency and war powers to the president, Congress has diminished its ability to resolve many of the nation's most critical issues. To reverse this diminution of power requires every member of Congress to be loyal to the institution of Congress rather than to the political party that helped elect them. Being loyal to the institution of Congress gives each member a stake in making Congress work as envisioned in the Constitution.

Congress must reclaim the emergency powers it delegated to the president before a dictator arises.

Nothing in our Constitution can be more explicit in intent than "All legislative Powers herein granted shall be vested in a Congress of the United States." Notwithstanding its constitutional mandate to legislate, Congress has delegated long-lasting emergency powers to the president to determine when an emergency starts and ends, and how to manage it.

Historically, emergency powers were limited to wartime and natural disasters. Today, however, Congress endows non-wartime presidents with the right to exercise wartime emergency powers to control citizens in domestic settings. The COVID-19 pandemic highlights how a president can use emergency powers to rule without Congress.

To address the COVID-19 pandemic, Presidents Trump and Biden relied on congressionally delegated emergency public health powers to comprehensively manage the many aspects of the pandemic, including hospitals, a nationwide ban on evictions, immigration, and student loans. When Congress and the public realized the extent to which they could be used, they became extraordinarily controversial. In a statement, Supreme Court Justice Gorsuch called the use of the COVID-19 emergency powers to address the immigration problem "the greatest intrusion on civil liberties in the peacetime history of this country. Executive officials across the country issued emergency decrees on a breathtaking scale," including lockdowns, closures, surveillance of churches, and the shuttering of schools. President Biden extended, by several years, President Trump's national emergency order on the COVID-19 pandemic by imposing mask and vaccine requirements on the nation while keeping the science supporting his proclamation secret. Biden also mandated that 84 million Americans subject to the Occupational Safety and Health Act either obtain a COVID-19 vaccine or submit to weekly testing.

In his second year in office, relying on the COVID-19 pandemic, Biden forgave tens of billions of interest payments of student loan debt. He asserted his Covid

emergency authority was based on the 2003 Higher
Education Relief Opportunities for Students Act ("HEROES
Act"). While the U.S. Supreme Court struck down the use of
the HEROES Act to forgive debt as a power grab beyond the
President's constitutional authority, Biden immediately took
another executive action to eliminate student debt. This time
he relied on the Higher Education Act of 1965. This second
attempt to disregard Congress and the Supreme Court
demonstrates how far a president will go to circumvent the
Constitution.

Of the 135 national emergency laws enacted by Congress;
the president is authorized under 96 of them to declare an
emergency by merely signing an emergency proclamation.
Once presidents are given such power, they can exercise it
until Congress takes it away.

Unfortunately, the term "National Emergency" is not
defined in federal law. The term "Emergency," is defined at
42 U.S.C. 5122(1), a section that deals with natural disasters
and cleanups, not events threatening the nation. Emergency
as defined in the U.S. Code "means any occasion or instance
for which, in the determination of the president, Federal
assistance is needed to supplement State and local efforts
and capabilities to save lives and to protect property and
public health and safety, or to lessen or avert the threat of a
catastrophe in any part of the United States."

The definition of "National Emergency" found in the
Merriam-Webster dictionary refers to events of a different
nature. It defines a national emergency as "a state of
emergency [an unforeseen circumstance needing immediate
action] resulting from a danger or threat of danger to a nation
from foreign or domestic sources and usually declared to be

in existence by governmental authority." It is a very subjective definition. Without a statutory definition of a "National Emergency," its meaning and scope are left to the dictionary, or worse, to the subjective interpretation of the president.

National Emergency laws terminate on the anniversary of their declaration unless the president notifies Congress of their continuation. The only legislative option for ending a national emergency is for Congress, by joint resolution, to terminate it. Since the president must sign joint resolutions, their repeal is difficult since Congress needs a two-thirds majority to override a likely presidential veto. Otherwise, these emergency powers are continuously available to the president. These laws allow U.S. Presidents to keep this nation in a perpetual national emergency. Presidents know how to use these powers; Congress needs to reclaim them.

In addition to health emergencies, other powers available to the president include the ability to control airports, industrial facilities, and any device capable of emitting electromagnetic radiation, including the nation's communications systems. The authority most used is the International Emergency Economic Powers Act ("IEEPA"). It authorizes the president to invoke emergency powers relating to U.S. national security, foreign policy, or the economy, including financial and commercial transactions. The IEEPA has been invoked 55 times. Sanctions can be imposed on individuals and countries, including freezing bank accounts and seizing assets. While there is a requirement that the threat be related to an activity in whole or part outside of the U.S., it is easy for a president to assert a foreign connection merely by accusation.

By enacting the National Emergencies Act, Congress gives all presidents the power to be a dictator at their chosen time. The only possible restraint is for Congress to repeal such laws. Only by acting as an institution that serves as a trustee of the Constitution can Congress find the votes from both political parties to repeal every emergency law.

Congress must reclaim the sole power to declare war.

Periodically there is a howling debate over the president's use of war powers, usually involving hostile actions against countries Congress has not declared war against. The political opposition party calls the actions unconstitutional and introduces a never-to-pass resolution, expressing "disapproval" so its members have media talking points. The president usually claims an imminent attack on the U.S. but rarely provides evidence of any serious threat. While the president is the commander-in-chief of the armed forces, only Congress has the power to declare war. Since the United States fights many undeclared wars, discussing how Congress abdicates this primary constitutional duty is necessary to appreciate how irrelevant Congress has become by delegating its war powers authority to the president.

The War Powers Act of 1973 was enacted to prevent another long but undeclared Viet Nam War situation. Under the Act, Congress grants the president, in the absence of a Declaration of War, limited powers to use force where the circumstances indicate imminent involvement in hostilities. When the president relies on this law, he must submit to Congress a report stating the reasons requiring armed forces, a statement of legal authority, and the scope and duration of the conflict. The submission of the information to Congress triggers a 60-day time limit on using force unless Congress extends the time.

Additionally, in 2001, Congress enacted the Authorized for Use of Military Force Against Terrorists ("AUMF"), which allows the president to use all necessary and appropriate force against nations, persons, or organizations that carried out the 2001 terrorist attacks against the U.S.

As a result of delegated authority under the War Powers Act and AUMF, a war is started by the president, not by a congressional Declaration of War. By relying on these delegated authorities, the president, as commander-in-chief, acts as if these powers are so broad, they authorize almost any hostile action against another country, for any period of time. Conversely, by Congress delegating such powers to the president, it has limited ability to stop a war initiated by the president unless it can pass a law to stop the war and has the support of two-thirds of the Congress to override a presidential veto or refusing to fund a war which may harm our troops.

As a nation, we are 234 years since the ratification of the Constitution. During that time, the U.S. has been at war for 138 years. Only five wars, totaling 32 years of war, were fought under a congressional declaration of war – the War of 1812, the Mexican War, the Spanish-American War, and World Wars I and II.

Examples of abuse of the War Powers Act.

President Reagan deployed troops to El Salvador but did not submit a report to Congress or comply with a withdrawal requirement. President George H.W. Bush sent troops to the Middle East and President Clinton sent troops to former

Yugoslavia. Both asserted they acted under UN authority and were not subject to congressional time limits.

Presidents George W. Bush, Obama, and Trump relied on AUMF at least 39 times for actions in 19 countries. Lawsuits were filed to enforce the notification provisions of the War Powers Act. The courts dismissed the lawsuits as political questions to be determined by the respective branches of government. The Supreme Court's reliance on the political question doctrine is an excellent example of how the courts have expanded presidential powers for over two centuries.

Afghanistan, our longest undeclared war, cost the nation $2.313 trillion, approximately $300 million daily for 20 years. The death toll was significant: 2,500 U.S. military, 4,000 civilians, and 69,000 Afghan military police. If Congress is unwilling to rescind the War Powers Act, it can always stop undeclared wars by refusing to appropriate money for its continuance. Congress never used its spending power authority to cut funds off to stop the war.

If Congress is to reclaim its role as the nation's lawmaker, it must reclaim its legislative authority over spending, emergencies, and wars. If Congress begins to reclaim these powers, it will realize the federal government, as structured, is too big and too complex to manage all the laws, policies, and programs it has accumulated over the last century. When it does, it will seek to form a governing structure that allows the federal government to manage issues of a genuine national and international nature and transfer domestic matters to the respective states. At that time, discussion over the devolution of power to the states will begin.

CHAPTER 12

Cleanup Task Two: Congress Must Separate Essential Government Services from Political Services and Gifts to Friends and Supporters

The confluence of major policy mistakes (massive debt, open borders, a two-tier system of justice, almost limitless regulations, efforts to restrict the use of fossil fuels, and a growing number of countries banding together to destroy our nation), is pushing the United States off the proverbial cliff.

While the federal government believes it should control all policies in the nation, that arrogance and lack of perspective establish its incompetence. The federal government must produce a plan for restructuring its spending and borrowing, if it is to get the nation's house in order. A successful reorganization requires an honest assessment of every national policy, all spending, taxes and tax credits, assets that can be sold, the elimination of excessive laws and regulations, federal lands that can be returned to the states, and grant, and loan programs that can be terminated. The result will allow Congress to evaluate which policies and assets are best managed by it or the states.

Business organizations facing systemic risks conduct comprehensive assessments of the troubles they face. It is now time for Congress to comprehensively analyze the viability, cost-benefit, and need of the tens of thousands of laws it has enacted and the regulations implementing those laws. When confronted with disaster, Congress and the federal government have successfully undertaken several comprehensive assessments and restructuring activities to preserve the economic viability of industries essential to the national economy. It is far past time for Congress to gain control over the mess it has created. It must restructure the federal government and address the national debt before the nation faces an existential crisis.

Perhaps the most successful assessment and eventual restructuring of an industry occurred in the mid-1970s when the Penn Central Railroad was in bankruptcy. The railroad was vital to the commerce of the nation. It transported a significant amount of the nation's products to the marketplace, including agriculture, farm animals, autos, large equipment, oil, gas, coal, steel, and most bulk shipments. As part of the restructuring, Congress and the executive branch examined the tens of thousands of miles of the railroad to determine what could be eliminated without harming the viability of the overall system. It also examined labor work rules, assets that could be sold, capability of management, and short-term financial needs. Congress reorganized the Penn Central Railroad into Conrail. Within a few years, the railroad became profitable and the federal government sold it back to the private market for a profit.

Similar reorganizations took place to rescue New York City and Chrysler Corporation from bankruptcy. The federal government has restructured the nation's automobile and banking industries several times.

Congress and the federal government can perform such an assessment on the many programs it has enacted, if it has the will to do it. The process for performing such an assessment is "oversight" and the "reauthorization" process. While Congress should be performing these duties on a regular basis, unfortunately, it does not. As noted in Chapter 13, Congress regularly funds thousands of laws that have not been reauthorized in years, some in decades, a clear illustration of its failure to perform its constitutional oversight responsibilities.

If it is the responsibility of citizens to ensure the federal government runs the country for the common good, not the good of politicians, they have failed. The federal government has spent more money than it brings in almost yearly since Calvin Coolidge was president in 1930. The American people now allow the federal government to spend $5-6 trillion annually for its operations. This amount is $1-2 trillion more than the federal government collects in taxes. Those amounts are always increasing. The nation's spending is now on overdrive, and there are no brakes. Our last seven presidents will have accumulated 97% of the estimated $36 trillion national debt by the end of the Biden administration in January, 2025.

On the asset side of the balance sheet, the federal government holds only $5.6 trillion of assets in cash, accounts receivable, loans receivable, and property, plant, and equipment. Its largest asset is $1.6 trillion of student loan debt, which the Biden administration wanted to forgive as a bribe to secure votes from college students. Such debt forgiveness would immediately add $1.6 trillion to the national debt.

Since regulations are considered laws by the federal government, the 200,000 plus complex regulations printed on almost10,000,000 pages of the Federal Register must be reduced. Fortunately, as Congress purges the nation of unneeded laws and devolves power to the states, the number of regulations will dramatically shrink since they no longer will be implementing federal laws, and will thereby be void.

With massive spending, millions of workers, an unknown number of laws and regulations to control every aspect of life, the federal government oozes incompetence. Not only is it *de facto* bankrupt, but it is also unable to control its borders, the essence of sovereignty. Its educational system, the core system for supporting future competition with the world, is in disarray. While the U.S. spends more money per student on education than any other country, it ranks 30th in math and 18th in reading on international assessments. Only 21% of its citizens believe it is going in the right direction. It is time to shrink the federal government for the benefit of the nation.

Members of Congress and the president should imagine their conference tables as merely kitchen tables where the family has been invited over for a discussion on finances.

The amount of information available to Congress for making smart fiscal policy decisions is significant, but seldom used. There are many excellent reports from the

Congressional Budget Office, the Government Accounting Office, and the Treasury, as well as dozens of think tanks. It is time Congress puts these materials to use.

A simple way to approach this task would be for each congressional committee to rank each program within its jurisdiction in order of priority. The budget and appropriation committees would work with the authorizing committees to ensure the highest-priority programs receive priority funding. The appropriation committees would work down the list until all tax revenue is expended. At that point, Congress would have to cease spending money on programs for which there is no longer any revenue. This approach will significantly eliminate the discretionary money to study insignificant concerns, such as shrimp on treadmills. If Congress wants to give agencies discretionary funds for non-essential projects, Congress would have to admit to the taxpayers it wants to borrow money to fund programs of dubious value. This kitchen-table process of spending only up to revenues received could save hundreds of billions of wasted dollars. It's just a common-sense approach.

Next, determine what assets are not needed.

Congress must compile a list of real assets (e.g., buildings, land, natural resources, and mineral rights). The assets should be prioritized, and only those needed for running the nation should be kept. Low-priority assets such as vacant buildings and land should be sold. The proceeds should be applied to pay off the nation's debt. Western lands, other than significant National Parks, should be returned to the states that want the land or Congress could authorize the land to be sold to the highest bidder.

Even after undertaking this right-sizing trauma, restructuring will only be just beginning. But at least Congress will have a spread sheet that allows it to begin evaluating its countless programs.

CHAPTER 13

Cleanup Task Three: Eight Easy Fixes for Spendthrifts to Reduce Federal Spending

It's time for Congress and the president to recognize they have a spending addiction. It is also time for the federal government to admit it cannot manage the nation's finances. In FY 2022, the United States collected $4.8 trillion in revenue and spent $6.32 trillion. Our federal government spent $1.52 trillion more in 2022 than taxpayers gave it to spend. The federal government has spent $34 trillion more than revenue collected. That is more money than the $25.46 trillion GDP of the nation. In human terms, the federal government would be considered an extremely fat and bloated organization. Congress needs simple solutions to reduce spending.

The prior chapter recommends the House and Senate have a family meeting over the nation's mismanaged finances to determine which programs are essential and which ones are not. Since Congress has been unable to manage the nation's finances for decades, it is unlikely it can complete this task. Democrats want a lot more spending while Republicans want just a little less spending. Neither party has put serious thought into reducing the national debt since the aftermath of World War II. Fortunately, there are a few actions Congress can undertake that would reduce federal spending by trillions with little creative thinking. All the hard work has been done. Congress only needs to follow the recommendations.

Eight easy fixes.

If "[the] journey of a thousand miles begins with one step," our federal government must start walking.

Fix 1. Do not fund laws that have not been authorized.

The most manageable set of budget cuts would be to refrain from funding laws that Congress has not authorized. "In FY 2021 appropriations, the Congressional Budget Office identified 1,068 authorizations of appropriations, stemming from 274 laws, totaling $432 billion, that expired before the beginning of the fiscal year 2022." Since House Rules prohibit funding programs it has not authorized, Congress need only follow its rules. Unfortunately, year after year Congress deems these laws reauthorized without any oversight and funds their implementation. If Congress does not have the time to hold reauthorization hearings on the viability of the programs, it should not fund them.

Fix 2. Review and vote on every expenditure of the Judgment Fund.

The Judgment Fund is the mother of all slush funds. It is now established as a permanent, indefinite, and unlimited congressional appropriation that is continuously available to pay money judgments entered against the United States and settlements of cases in or likely to be in litigation with the United States. The fund is so secret that Congress no longer even debates what the amounts are for. The amounts are appropriated, no matter the amount. The Department of the Treasury pays the claims upon the receipt of the paperwork. The Judgment Fund is the fund that President Obama used to deliver $1.7 billion in cash to Iran as a bribe to sign the nuclear deal. The Obama administration described the deal as a return of Iranian money held by the U.S. In actuality, the U.S. held only $400 million of Iranian assets and the Judgment Fund paid Iran $1.3 billion in interest on the monies the U.S. held. Why should our government officials have billions in a secret fund to cover up illegal activity? Having Congress approve each judgment and settlement as it did before 1956, the U.S. could save taxpayers tens of billions of dollars.

Supporters of the Judgment Fund process argue it would be unworkable for Congress to review every payment since there are likely thousands. Such a position ignores the fact that in its appropriations process, Congress specifically votes to fund thousands of identified programs. A review of the Judgment Fund process would be simple; all the payments would be disclosed in the legislation brought to the floor. Every member would know what is being paid and could force a debate to strike any item just as in any other appropriations bill.

The real reason Congress does not want to disclose the items being paid out of the Judgment Fund is to avoid embarrassment over some of the payments for improper activities and lawsuits against members of Congress.

Fix 3. Follow and implement GAO's Generally Accepted Accounting Principles ("GAAP").

Congress mandates its Government Accounting Office ("GAO") to perform a Generally Accepted Principles and Practices ("GAAP") analysis of federal spending and assets and to provide recommendations to ensure the financial reporting by an agency is transparent and consistent. Every member of Congress should read these reports on how our money is managed and should implement its findings. One specific GAO recommendation is for the federal government to address government-wide improper payments, estimated to be $247 billion.

Fix 4. Government must operate only for a public purpose.

The federal government has been giving away money to private parties since the start of the Republic. Moreover, the courts have made it clear that Congress determines the general welfare. To address the excesses of gifts to private individuals, Congress must stop "cold turkey" giving gifts to friends and other private entities. Chapter 20 identifies a few of the trillions in gifts to friends and private entities that could be eliminated.

To paraphrase a quote attributed to Senator Evert Dirksen when he cautioned Congress about reckless spending, "A trillion here, a trillion there, and pretty soon you're talking real money."

Fix 5. Re-constitute the Joint Committee on Reduction of Non-Essential Federal Expenditures from 1941 to 1974 ("Joint Committee").

This Joint Committee was established after World War II to recommend ways to reduce a massive federal budget. Its goal was to identify non-essential spending. While the Joint Committee was only a study committee for the thirty- three years of its existence, many of its recommendations were acted upon by the authorizing and appropriations committees. With the inability of Congress to control spending and the states being unable to persuade enough states to call for a Constitutional Convention to adopt a Balanced Budget amendment to the U.S. Constitution, an alternative mechanism for controlling spending must be found. Creating a joint committee similar to the original joint-committee could be a viable option, with one essential change, both houses of Congress must be required to vote on all its recommendations. This process will create fiscal accountability.

Fix 6. Enact a Base Realignment and Closure Commission ("BRAC") that applies to general appropriations.

Due to political pressure to locate the military bases in numerous congressional districts, the U.S. constructed an excess of bases but could not close unneeded bases due to strong local constituent support. To address the situation, Congress established BRAC, giving the Commission power to identify unnecessary bases and make recommendations to

Congress. Congress could apply the BRAC process to identify unneeded expenditures. The key to BRAC's success is that its recommendations to Congress became law unless Congress passed a Resolution of Disapproval and the president signed it.

Since this approach involves a significant constitutional function, spending, Congress should not delegate away any of its constitutional authority. To guarantee congressional involvement, the BRAC-type commission should make recommendations to the Appropriations Committees of the House and Senate. It would be up to those committees to determine how the recommendations should be addressed by Congress. Conversely, if Congress so fears its constituents, it could again avoid responsibility for managing the nation by establishing a BRAC type process that allows all the cuts to become law unless it passes a Resolution of Disapproval and the president signs it.

Fix 7. Establish a position in every agency to identify unnecessary expenditures.

Periodically, presidents have established agency positions to ensure certain activities were more effectively implemented. When the recycling industry was in its infancy, president George H.W. Bush issued an Executive Order to promote cost-effective waste reduction and recycling programs in federal agencies. To ensure agency implementation, the president required agencies to appoint a Federal Recycling Coordinator.

A similar position could be established for identifying and reducing unnecessary expenditures by federal agencies. The person would report directly to the head of the agency.

The president should mandate all expenditure reduction reports, and agency actions on the reports be made public. Each coordinator should recommend at 10% reduction in agency expenditures in every administration. The official should receive a bonus for meeting the target.

Fix 8. Enact a fair, simple tax code that raises money to operate the government rather than legislating social policy.

Fortunately, most of the work to achieve this fix, including the IRS Forms, was prepared in 1913 and is still available.

The current complex tax code invites under-reporting and manipulation, whereas a simple tax code fosters greater participation and prevents large-scale manipulation encouraged by complexity. This simple solution is to repeal the 8-million-word IRS tax code and replace it with the 1913- four-page Form 1040, having few deductions and low rates but requiring everyone to pay some tax, including the wealthiest and the poorest. Another benefit of this simple approach is it captures a greater amount of tax owed by making it harder to hide income. The IRS defines the tax gap as the difference between actual taxes owed for a given year and the amount paid. The gap is caused by the under-reporting of income, non-filing, and tax evasion. While the exact amount is unknown, the IRS estimates it to range from $574 to $700 billion annually.

Congress presently has a few, easy to implement solutions to save trillions over the next few years. While Congress lives in fear of voters, it lacks an understanding that its mismanagement may cause the nation to collapse.

CHAPTER 14

Cleanup Task Four: Get the Bureaucracy Under Control with Term Limits and RIFs

In the mid-1940s, as the world approached the end of WWII, Winston Churchill is credited with saying, "Never let a good crisis go to waste." While Churchill was likely referring to the alliance between Roosevelt, Stalin, and himself to form the United Nations, the popular use of the statement is that a crisis provides an opportunity to do what could not be done before the crisis. The federal bureaucracy aggressively used the COVID-19 pandemic crisis to establish working from home as a right of employment. The polite name for such work is "telework."

Congress should now recognize that a work-at-home bureaucracy, for the first time in one hundred and fifty years, provides the opportunity to restructure what has become an annual $136 billion compensation expense for a civil service that imposes $2 trillion in regulatory costs on taxpayers. Since federal workers have already established that they no longer work in federal offices, it is time for the Congress to determine how many federal workers are needed and where.

Restructuring will reduce expensive office space, pollution, and promote diversity.

The bureaucrats argue working from home reduces traffic congestion and allows GSA to downsize office space between 20% to 50% of post-pandemic levels while reducing greenhouse gases. Moreover, workers argue it saves energy, increases worker productivity by having fewer distractions, and opens the nationwide talent pool to federal employment. Workers also argue it promotes greater diversity, equity, and inclusion in government recruitment. One study finds "remote work is now the status quo for much of the federal government." The same study noted, "... 6 in 10 [workers] would take a pay cut" if allowed to work from home.

The studies on remote work support reorganizing the bureaucracy for the next century. Since the existing system is based on the Pendleton Act of 1883 and the Civil Service Reform Act of 1978, the bureaucracy seriously needs reform to function efficiently in a more diverse and technological society. Today's civil service has literally lifetime appointments. Federal employees are fired at the rate of 0.55%, a rate so low that deaths outnumber firings. Two significant agencies have had zero discharges in several years. In addition to job security, the Congressional Budget Office found pay and benefits for bureaucrats was 47% more than the combined pay and benefits in the private sector. A Cato Institute study put the number at 80% more than the private sector. The average federal worker receives $123,160 in pay and benefits compared to $69,901 in the private sector.

A successful reorganization of the federal workplace will open the civil service to a dynamic nationwide talent pool. Moreover, the transition of federal power to the states will create local employment opportunities in all states.

How does Congress achieve this reorganization?

Unfortunately, the U.S. Supreme Court ruled that a bureaucrat can only be dismissed from federal employment after a trial-type hearing. This ruling makes discharging an individual bureaucrat almost impossible. It leaves nearly two million civil servants in control of the spin on the information given to elected officials. In foreign affairs, these bureaucrats have the ability to replace the president's policy with policies adopted by the interagency working groups they control.

These "lifers" fundamentally change the role of the president. Article II requires the president to execute the laws of the U.S., yet the president controls only 4,000 appointments out of 2 million civil service positions. 99.8% of the bureaucracy beats to its own drummer, and the Supreme Court protects its music. Many highly paid elites believe "the public knows little or nothing" about the nation's issues so, let the bureaucrats reign.

Over time, the public lost trust in the government. In 1958, almost 75% of Americans trusted the government. In 2022, only 20% of Americans trusted the government.

The worst part of the bureaucracy is that it hides behind statistically flawed, faux evaluations, giving 99.5% of the 2 million federal employees a "fully successful" rating or above. Of the 2 million bureaucrats, only 0.1% received unacceptable ratings.

As Congress struggles with a massive national debt, an unresponsive bureaucracy, and a polarized society, it needs to have an efficient bureaucracy that works to achieve the policy goals established by Congress, not the personal goals of each bureaucrat. To achieve this redirection, Congress must restructure the bureaucracy, and it cannot do it one position at a time which will trap it in countless trials, as mandated by the Supreme Court. Congress has two viable alternatives for reorganizing the federal bureaucracy.

Term Limits for Bureaucrats.

If Congress is to reorganize the bureaucracy, it must place term limits on bureaucrats, perhaps eight years of service. Term limits would have three significant benefits for our country. First, it would break bureaucratic control of government by eliminating the power imbalance between elected officials whose service can regularly be limited by citizens and an unaccountable bureaucracy that can hold jobs for life. Second, with term limits, more Americans can serve their country and reap the rewards of a federal job. Finally, term limits would reduce the number of bureaucrats qualifying for massive federal pensions and health benefits, now representing a $3.5 trillion unfunded liability.

There are also substantial social and economic benefits of term-limiting bureaucrats. With open positions, the federal government can hire talent based on ability, knowledge, and skills from every part of the country. These new employees could be in rural and low-income areas with few federal workers. One study estimated that 20% of federal positions (approximately 400,000 jobs) could be done effectively

anywhere in the U.S. The study also finds that a more
distributed workforce can combat "widening geographic
inequality."

As work is created in economically depressed areas, it
will generate economic opportunities for these areas by
attracting businesses wanting to provide services to the
federal operations located there. By working in lower-cost
areas, the federal government can reduce its cost-of-living
adjustments from 30.5% in high-cost areas like Washington,
DC, to 16% in most of the U.S. While the federal
government saves money, so do the employees living in low-
cost areas.

More importantly, with federal employees spread
throughout the U.S., the federal government will be closer to
the governed. Citizens in every part of the U.S. will be able
to interact with federal employees and understand them
better. Moreover, by being distributed over 50 states, the
federal employees will learn about the needs of Americans
in the fly-over country and state and local government. Over
time this should help restore trust in the government.

By vacating federal office space and working remotely
federal employees have already put this process in motion.
A recent report from the Government Accountability Office
confirms that many federal workers have moved out of
Washington, DC and do not want to return to the central
offices. Seventeen federal office buildings in downtown
D.C., as recently as September 2023, have occupancy rates
of 25% and some less. These vacant buildings cost billions
of dollars to maintain. As for workers, an internal survey
characterized a return to office policy as "unworkable,
indicating they would look for a new job or retire as a result

of it." Moreover, the federal government presently pays a substantial wage premium for workers who are assigned to work in Washington, DC, but who are not working there. As to the benefits of finding qualified workers throughout the U.S., The National Science Foundation's liberal telework policy has allowed it "to hire brilliant scientists who live all over the country-from California to Colorado to Florida-and to retain staff who moved out of the Washington, D.C., area for personal reasons."

The situation is clear. Federal workers do not want to work in Washington, DC. Mostly for cost and congestion reasons. Brilliant talent can be recruited from across the U.S. to work for the federal government remotely. Federal buildings have high vacancy rates and the unions are negotiating for the workers to have permanent telework rights. In light of the cost to maintain millions of square feet of unoccupied office space and to pay workers a premium wage for working in Washington, DC, it is time for the federal government to move a substantial part of the federal workforce out of the very expensive nation's capital and spread it across the nation. Iowa and Nebraska have more people with knowledge of farming than DC will ever have. Most large cities have more substantial experience with low-income housing than does the Department of Housing and Urban Development. The list could go on agency by agency, but the point is clear. Washington, DC is not the center of all knowledge in the U.S.

Reductions in force ("RIFs") due to the transfer of federal programs to the states or their elimination.

While individual federal employees can only be term-limited by an agency for poor performance after a trial-type hearing, they are not protected from a Congress that reduces an agency budget or restructures an agency. Budget cuts mean employees can be laid off for large-scale changes in an agency structure. In the language of the federal government, this process is a RIF. When a RIF occurs, the federal government has long-standing procedures and detailed regulations that must be followed as part of the reduction in force. RIF regulations allow some employees to move into different federal workforce positions based on specific criteria concerning tenure, veteran preferences, and performance ratings. Since the RIF process is already in place, the federal government has a mechanism to deal with a large-scale budget reduction or changes due to devolving federal power to the states. If the RIF is part of the devolution of federal powers to the states, Congress could incentivize the states to hire many of the federal employees subject to the RIF.

The federal government only needs the bureaucracy if it implements congressional policies. If not, Congress has the power to RIF it.

The real question is whether Congress dares to take on the unions that protect the bureaucracy. With the many problems facing the nation, a bloated, non-functioning bureaucracy is not helping the country. Term limits on the bureaucracy, telework and RIFs resulting from the devolution of power to the states allow Congress wide latitude to re-make a bureaucracy that works for taxpayers, not itself. These changes should be part of any government-wide restructuring effort undertaken by Congress.

CHAPTER 15

Cleanup Task Five: If the Institution of Congress Cannot Clean Up Its Mess, One House of Congress Has the Power to Do It

The 2023 drama in Congress over a debt ceiling default, budget negotiations, the continuous threat of government shutdowns, the ouster of the Speaker of the House Kevin McCarthy ("Speaker McCarthy"), and the difficulty in electing a new Speaker, is the nation's first peek at what will be a long-running drama over a national debt that will eventually destroy the nation, if not reduced. Historically, cooperation on fiscal mismanagement meant appropriating more money for the government to spend. That type of cooperation is what created the problem; a national debt of 120% of the nation's GDP, the funding of thousands of unauthorized laws, fostering the issuance of hundreds of thousands of regulations, the growth of the administrative state, the assumption of hundreds of billions of dollars of off-budget liabilities, and the funding of trillions in off-budget wars.

President Biden wanted an increase in the debt ceiling to keep government growing. A majority of Republicans voted with the Democrats to increase the debt ceiling to avoid a debt default. Seventy-one Republicans, mostly Freedom Caucus members, voted against raising the debt ceiling. They wanted to use the debt ceiling as a mechanism to reduce the nation's national debt. As usual in the hocus pocus of Washington deal-making, the debt ceiling was increased and theoretically some spending restraints were agreed upon.

The deal allowed both parties to again claim victory. The Democrats got to claim they avoided cuts in domestic programs. Republicans got to claim they increased military and veterans spending. On the larger issue of the nation's increasing national debt, both parties supported the elimination of the debt ceiling limit until after the next presidential election. In simple terms, on a bipartisan basis Congress and the president agreed to spend an additional $2 trillion it does not have over the next two years.

Members of the Freedom Caucus believed they were deceived by Speaker McCarthy on the deficit reduction parts of the debt ceiling debate. Due to the failure of the Appropriations Committees in the House and Senate to finalize the funding of the government by the September 30, 2023 fiscal year deadline, the Freedom Caucus had another legislative opening to again seek large reductions in federal spending. The president and Democrats wanted Congress to pass a Continuing Resolution to fund the government to at least last year's levels, which were very inflated due to the significant pandemic spending. The Freedom Caucus strenuously objected to a Continuing Resolution since it places the federal government on an automatic pilot at a high level of spending.

Speaker McCarthy, fearful of a government shutdown, publicly protested he was acting in America's best interest by putting a relatively clean Continuing Resolution on the floor to keep the government open for another 45 days. The Speaker took the Continuing Resolution to the floor. The Republicans needed some Democratic support to pass the Continuing Resolution. Most of the Democrats supported the Speaker since they wanted the higher levels of funding. Again, a large minority of 90 Republicans voted against the clean Continuing Resolution. It passed with a majority of both parties voting for it.

A few members of the Freedom Caucus believed Speaker McCarthy had broken his promises to keep spending under control. Within days, Congressman Matt Gaetz filed a motion to vacate the Speaker's chair. The Republican Speaker, having only a five-seat majority in the House, could not afford to lose the votes of more than five Republican members. Eight Republican members voted to vacate the chair.

If Speaker McCarthy was to retain his Speakership, he would again need Democratic support. In the legislative debates over the debt ceiling and the Continuing Resolutions to fund the government, the Democrats voted with the Speaker since both measures helped achieve the increased spending goals of the Democrats. When it came to keeping a Republican, Kevin McCarthy, in the Speaker's chair, all the Democrats voted with the eight Freedom Caucus Republican members to remove Speaker McCarthy, thereby temporarily putting the House in chaos.

While the House of Representatives elected a new speaker several weeks later, the turmoil focuses on a more serious issue; Congress has failed to control spending for decades. It cannot even follow its own rules and pass the twelve appropriations bills by the October 1 start of the fiscal year. The last time Congress passed all twelve appropriations as separate appropriation bills was 1996. Generally, Congress keeps the federal government running by passing a massive 4,000-page Omnibus Appropriation. This procedure denies legislators sufficient time to read the text of what they are voting on. Alternately, Congress passes Continuing Resolutions that fund the government at a prior year's level. By failing to comply with its own rules, Congress ensures that the federal government remains an unsupervised behemoth by spending trillions of taxpayer dollars annually, with little review of the policies citizens pay for.

If both Houses of Congress continue the gross mismanagement of the taxpayer's money, the federal government will eventually collapse the United States. While Congress has proven it is unable to manage the nation's money, it must always be remembered, if just one House of Congress wants to stop spending, and start a path to fiscal sanity, it has the power to do it.

How is such power possible when laws must be passed by the House and Senate and signed by the president?

There is a real but rarely used power that allows a majority of just one House of Congress to control the nation's budget and the size of government. All one House of Congress, likely the House of Representatives, needs do is to refuse to appropriate money to run the parts of the government that it deems unworkable or not carrying out congressional intent. By exercising this power, one House of Congress has a veto over wasteful government spending.

How would this process work?

Under our Constitution "No Money shall be drawn from the Treasury, but in Consequence of Appropriations made by Law." This power can be used to authorize more spending or be used to reduce spending and the national debt.

For Congress to spend more of the taxpayer's money, it must appropriate the new money by enacting a law that requires the approval of both Houses of Congress and a presidential signature. To spend no money, however, one House of Congress merely needs to do nothing. No provision in the Constitution gives the power to anyone to force Congress to spend money. Moreover, as an institution, Congress is the only branch of government that controls the nation's purse. One House of Congress can close that purse.

Additionally, under Article I, section 7 of the U.S. Constitution, all bills for raising revenue must originate in the House of Representatives. Moreover, only Congress can increase the amount of borrowing undertaken by the federal government. By electing a majority in either House of Congress that support achieving fiscal sanity and smaller government, one House would have the power to block the enactment of new revenue streams and more borrowing to support a bigger government.

It is clear that no matter how big or powerful the federal government becomes, a majority of one House of Congress can rein it in if it has courage to do so. Election after election, candidates promise to shrink government, but that never occurs. The federal government always grows since the two major parties support more and more spending and borrowing. Fortunately, every two years, the American people have an opportunity to check the federal government's power by electing a Congress that will bring sanity to the nation's financial management.

PART IV

Restructuring a Republic to Restore Trust in Government

CHAPTER 16

Principles for Restructuring a Failed Federal Government

The restructuring of businesses in the United States is common. Unfortunately, we seldom think about restructuring our government or how it could be accomplished. Government just grows, debt increases, new wars start, regulations flourish, its friends are rewarded, and its enemies punished.

All this political churn accomplishes in a competitive world is to reduce trust in government and diminish the living standards of citizens. People live with the poor government until there is a crisis. It is likely too late to make the government trustworthy to citizens at that moment. An unaccountable government is dangerous path forward. The American citizens cannot continue to accept a failed federal government. It is time to restructure the federal government to make it work for citizens. Only then will there be trust in the government.

While the government does not have the same functions

as a corporation, the two have one fundamental common goal; both must function for the benefit of those they were established to serve. By having a common goal, the starting point is clear. There needs to be an analysis of the fundamental problems that interfere with the ability of the government to get its job done for its people. The basic principles are:

Do not delay the restructuring.

The longer the delay, the greater risk of failure by letting the problems become more unmanageable. At some point there are fewer options for a successful restructuring.

There must be an honest assessment of the federal government's problems and the resources available for solving them.

The significant problems and the tools for addressing them must be identified, including accurate financials, realistic inventories, the sources of existing and potential revenues, long-term liabilities, a list of possible programs and policies that can be eliminated, assets that can be sold, the identification of future needs, and the costs of managing them.

This assessment will help identify the nation's top priorities. Indeed, national defense and economic security are at the top of the list. What is on the rest of the list: a sound banking system, protection of the sovereign borders, Social Security, and many others. An honest assessment will lay the foundation for a long-lasting strategy to create a government that provides the services its citizens need and the elimination of non-essential programs.

Reduce complexity and promote transparency.

Reducing complexity and promoting transparency are essential to the process of restructuring. Most significantly, they allow citizens to understand what the government is doing to serve their needs. They form a foundation of trust in government. Also, they are a guide for lowering operating costs, increasing job performance, reducing duplication, removing barriers to economic development, and dealing with the government.

Hold the individuals managing programs accountable for their success or failure.

In our current federal government, there is no accountability. Our many federal cabinet officers and other political appointees are figureheads, not managers. The decision-makers are on the White House staff. The Senate does not confirm any of those individuals. This invisible power structure must be eliminated or subject to Senate confirmation, to ensure Congress can perform oversight by hearing from the individuals having decision-making control over the programs. The better solution would be for the president's cabinet secretaries and other Senate confirmed officials to have decision-making control over the programs under their jurisdiction. The other managers are those in the civil service. They hold jobs for life, even when there is a severe failure in program management. At the start of each budget cycle, every cabinet secretary and civil service manager must be informed of the goals of every program under their management. They must be responsible for achieving those goals. Sanctions must exist for poor and failing performances, including termination.

There must be a clear plan for eliminating programs, policies, personnel, and expenditures that do not achieve the goals established by Congress.

Eliminating unneeded or non-performing programs and personnel is essential to right-sizing government. Every dollar given to the federal government must be effectively managed to achieve the needs of the citizens paying for the federal government. All non-performing programs, policies and expenditures must be eliminated.

There must be a clear plan for transferring to the states those federal programs that can be more effectively managed at a state or local level of government.

By bringing programs closer to the people they serve, there will be more trust in government as citizens understand what the government is doing and why. Achieving an accountable government trusted by the people is the essence of devolution.

Applying these principles is a more difficult task. Before any restructuring can occur, we must all ask: what are the essential attributes needed by government officials to build trust in them as officials and the programs they manage?

CHAPTER 17

The Constitution Mandates Government Officials Serve as Fiduciaries, Not Politicians

The writings of John Locke, Edmond Burke, and James Madison reflect their fundamental belief that since no power is granted to our representatives as individuals, all officials must function as fiduciaries, not politicians.

A fiduciary is a person who has a duty, created by a voluntary undertaking, to act for the benefit of another in matters connected with such effort. Government officials voluntarily seek and assume positions in our government. They freely take an oath to support the Constitution. When they voluntarily assume the responsibility of managing our government, we entrust them with our money, property, liberty, the fair implementation of our laws, and the defense of our country. They must act in accordance with the trust we have placed in them.

Government officials must never act for personal benefit or the benefit of the political party that supports them. Such actions are a breach of their fiduciary duty to the institution in which they serve. Elected officials have significant responsibilities that, if not properly executed, can create massive abuses that significantly harm the nation.

Government officials having fiduciary obligations is a controversial topic. More than a few well-crafted law review articles argue that the fiduciary duty standard cannot be easily transferred from trust or corporate law to public law. These scholars argue that, in the public arena, there is simply no way to determine who is the beneficiary of a government official's duty of loyalty.

These law review articles provide excellent straw-men examples of the unworkability of imposing a fiduciary relationship between government officials and the diverse laws to be administered, constituents, and institutions to be served. They argue since there is no consensus on what interests are to be protected, a trust relationship cannot be imposed on elected officials. The critics' reason is that since validly enacted laws, regulations, and Executive Orders are constitutional, the exercise of a fiduciary duty must encompass all governmental actions, or the fiduciary duty cannot be imposed on the government official.

This "too much complexity argument" misses the critical point by jumping to the conclusion that to be a fiduciary, the government official must be a fiduciary to every constituent for all validly enacted laws, regulations, orders, and other government actions. That is not what our Constitution mandates. Our Constitution is clear; the Oaths Clause refers to the framework of the Constitution. As such, all actions must be consistent with its structure of limited government held in check by officials defending the separation of powers between the three branches of government. Therefore, the fiduciary duty merely reaffirms what the Oaths Clause imposes – loyalty must be to the structure of our Constitution and the institution in which one serves, and not to every constituent. It's this "structure of the government," especially the separation of powers, that Chief Justice Marshall alludes to in *McCulloch v Maryland*, as being able to control the abuses of government.

Our Constitution establishes three separate institutions of government to protect us by having each branch check the powers of the other branches of government. When this system of checks and balances fails, it is a breach of fiduciary duty by those officials in our several branches of government who allow the failure to occur. An example of a breach of duty is when a president exercises unlawful legislative powers and the members of his party in Congress refuse to check the presidential abuse of power.

In theory, the Constitution works well. In practice, however, the constitutional mandate of separation of powers is regularly abused by our elected officials. When members of Congress and federal officers ignore their duties to defend the separation of powers and their duties under the Constitution, these members function as Republicans or Democrats, not as trustees of the Constitution. Evidence of this breach of fiduciary duty is illustrated daily by the almost near unanimous party-line voting by members of Congress on major legislation. Another example is the willingness of members of Congress from the president's party to protect the president when he improperly withholds information needed by Congress to perform its oversight responsibilities.

When political parties control the power structure, they

replace the institutional responsibilities of the three branches of government with the goals of the political party. When these types of actions occur, citizens have their rights greatly diminished. Citizens are then only protected by political parties and cannot depend on the respective government institutions for protection.

Citizens need to continually remind themselves that political parties are nothing more than special interest organizations created for one purpose - to control the government of the United States for the benefit of the party and its members. Political parties are so successfully organized that two political parties control all aspects of government. When one party controls all branches of government, it enacts whatever laws or regulations it wishes, even when its enactments are unconstitutional. When one party controls the presidency and one House of Congress, the politicians in Congress from the president's party can block the opposing party from checking the illegal actions of the president. In these instances, the institutions of our government are made irrelevant by politics.

While there are many examples of how political power trumps institutional power, what is clear is that if members of Congress gave all their loyalty to the institution of Congress, they would prevent much of the political overreach by the executive or judicial branches. The same would be true if members of the executive and judicial branches served as fiduciaries and not as politicians, by constantly checking the powers of Congress.

Under the U.S. Constitution, citizens are to be protected by three government institutions. When our elected representatives give their loyalty to the political party rather than the institution in which they serve, the people of the nation are protected only by Republicans or Democrats, depending on who is in power.

CHAPTER 18

Trust in Government Depends on Transparency and Truth-Telling

The U.S. federal government can only survive with the trust of the people it claims to serve. Individuals controlling government through misinformation, lies, deceit, and secrecy undermine every aspect of being a Republic.

The federal government, for decades, has had citizens living in information confusion, and conspiracy theories. Information clutter explains why only two in ten Americans trust Washington to do the right thing. Distinguishing between good and bad quality information should never be difficult when the information comes from our government. Unfortunately, the federal government only disseminates information that fits its narrative, which it continuously attempts to impose on citizens as reality.

It should not be surprising that the federal government's growing power, size, and cost force it to continuously justify its existence. Since it cannot explain the value citizens receive for the trillions of dollars sent to the federal government, it seeks to baffle citizens with propaganda. Four hundred thirty-eight federal agencies employ over 1.9 million civilians. Millions of federal contractors support these federal employees at a cost of $694 billion. More than forty percent of the federal workforce are government contractors. A New York University study estimates that the true size of the federal workforce is 9.1 million workers. Additionally, the federal government co-ops states to administer federal programs the federal government lacks authority to administer. In 2022, the federal government purchased $1.2 trillion of state services.

Today, this massive collection of unelected federal officials has over 200,000 regulations that imposed $1.9 trillion of regulatory costs in 2021. These costs are in addition to the $6 trillion Congress appropriates to federal agencies for general operations.

This collection of employees, contractors, regulations, related costs, permit requirements, and adjudications is called the "Administrative State."

Little, unfortunately, has been done to control the Administrative State since its birth in the 1930s. It just expands. Why is it so uncontrollable? Is it just too big to be managed? While Congress and the president can always shrink it, that never happens since all branches of the federal government benefit significantly by its expansion. The federal government's goal is for the Administrative State to secure maximum control over citizens. By having control over citizens, every member of the federal government is more secure in their privileged status as a "ruler of the people."

Can the Administrative State be managed, reformed, or made to comply with duly enacted laws?

The Administrative State cannot be controlled.

The first and only successful effort by Congress to control the Administrative State occurred in 1946 with the enactment of the Administrative Procedure Act ("APA"). Congress was so concerned with the 157 regulations issued by federal agencies that it imposed procedures for issuing and enforcing rules. Congress mandated agencies to provide the public with information on the necessity of their proposals and to ensure public participation in the process. Congress also provided for judicial review of all agency regulations to ensure agencies were faithfully implementing the laws they were administering. Even with the APA's restrictions on agency rulemakings, federal agencies have issued several hundred thousand regulations since 1946.

The courts were not only as ineffective as Congress in limiting the power of the Administrative State, but it is the courts that engineered its growth. Instead of providing needed oversight of agency actions to ensure compliance with the intent of Congress, the federal courts significantly expanded agency power by allowing agencies to escape congressional oversight.

Rather than holding agencies strictly to the intent of Congress, the courts granted deference to agency interpretations of the law if there was any vagueness in the statute. Judicial deference became the fuel for growing executive power and, eventually, agency lawmaking power. Deference allows the president to diminish Congress by tipping the scales in favor of executive branch interpretations of the laws passed by Congress. Unless the opposition party to the president has the votes to pass a law overriding an agency regulation, the laws made through the regulatory process stand, notwithstanding the intent of Congress.

Placing limits on federal agency power failed.

Congress complains about agencies making law by regulation but does little to change it.

Congress has yet to substantively amend the APA in the 76 years since its enactment.

From 2015 to 2018, (the 114th and 115th Congresses), the House Committee on the Judiciary seriously attempted to reform the APA and, by implication, the Administrative State through the Regulatory Accountability Act ("RAA"). The RAA sought to reform the rulemaking process to ensure final rules were based on sound facts and law and implemented congressional intent. The House passed the RAA. The Senate voted it out of committee; however, Senate Republican leadership refused to bring it to the floor. This effort was Congress' first and last serious attempt to reform the Administrative State since passing the APA in 1946.

Congress has shown a lack of interest and an inability to control federal agencies. Or, perhaps Congress secretly views lawmaking by federal agencies as a benefit. Agency lawmaking by regulation allows Congress to blame agencies for matters adversely impacting their constituents while not having to be accountable for the consequences.

Even when Congress mandates the Administrative State provide the public with good-quality information, it refuses.

The best illustration of the federal government's intent to misinform and deceive the American public is its refusal to comply with the Information Quality Act ("IQA"), which is found at section 515 of the Fiscal Year 2001 Treasury and General Government Appropriations Act.

The IQA is designed to foster trust in government information. The IQA requires the Office of Management of Budget ("OMB") to ensure and maximize "… the quality, objectivity, utility, and integrity of information (including statistical information) disseminated by federal agencies."

In 2002, OMB issued detailed guidelines defining the IQA terms. Information disseminated by the government was to be accurate (precise, complete, and unbiased); useful to intended users; and possessing integrity (protected from manipulation). OMB also set forth a correction process for citizens, including experts, to challenge data inaccuracies. For influential scientific information, there must be a "high degree of transparency about data and methods to facilitate the reproducibility of such information by qualified third parties." IQA procedures were designed to build trust in government information by following a modified scientific method of testing and reproducibility of data.

Information is "any communication or representation of knowledge such as facts or data, in any medium or form." Dissemination of information to the public included agency distribution of information to the public. While the IQA does not cover opinions, the agency must clearly identify opinions when communicated to the public.

Had IQA guidelines been followed during the COVID-19 crisis, the federal government would have provided the public with more useful information. Government-issued mandates provided little supporting information and never provided the level of uncertainty of the vaccines or any FDA test results. By not following IQA guidelines during the almost daily COVID-19 briefings, misinformation and opinions were regularly stated as facts without supporting documentation or being noted as opinions. As a result, citizens were forced to live in lockdowns, masks were mandated, schools closed, causing massive learning losses, and natural immunity was deemed a conspiracy theory.

Both the Trump and Biden administrations waffled between presidential statements seeking evidence-based information on COVID-19's origins and the unequivocal public statements of the federal government's leading propagandist, Dr. Fauci, who pronounced it came from an animal. After several years of delay, the FBI and Energy Department informed the public "the Covid pandemic most likely arose from a [Wuhan] laboratory leak," not from animals, highlighting the difficulty in believing federal government health information.

The daily federal public guidance consisted of Fauci communicating inconsistent health-related information. First, he told the public, "There's no reason to be walking around with a mask." A few weeks later, he supported universal masking. Subsequently, he endorsed double masking. As independent scientists offered contrary views, Fauci and his boss, Francis Collins, formulated a press strategy to discredit the credibility of their leading critics as conspiracy theorists.

Federal misinformation fostered a state of fear. In depositions, Fauci could not identify any study he relied upon to support his conflicting policy pronouncements. And when asked direct questions about his knowledge of the virus's origins or the tests supporting his conclusions, he "could not remember." Eventually, state Attorneys General successfully obtained a court injunction against the Centers for Disease Control concerning the legality of Fauci's mask mandates.

Such misinformation harmed public health. A Lancet study finds public trust in government is vital to effectively implementing public health measures. Yet, the federal government, for several years, intentionally communicated public health misinformation.

The federal government refuses to provide good quality data to the public.

From the moment OMB issued the IQA guidelines in 2002, almost every federal agency fought to undermine its implementation. Agencies argued OMB's guidelines are discretionary. DOJ supported the agencies in court filings.

The public filed lawsuits against agencies to implement the IQA guidelines and to correct inaccurate information. These efforts failed. The courts avoided interpreting the substance of the statute by holding private parties lacked standing to enforce IQA requirements. The federal courts gave agencies complete discretion on the type of information disseminated to the public. With strong resistance from the federal government, the IQA drifted into obscurity. It is incredible that on public health issues, the court did not recognize that citizens can be directly injured by public health misinformation; as such they should have had standing to sue.

If the IQA had been implemented during COVID-19, federal agencies would have been limited to disseminating only reliable, consistent, reproducible information or would have had to disclose the agency did not have supporting data. Under the IQA, Fauci would have had to inform the public that his daily statements were mere opinions, or worse, talking points for a television performance. The American people would have known the truth, which would have allowed them to seek guidance from knowledgeable health professionals.

Government misinformation is propaganda. Government misinformation permeates our society, from climate change to nutrition to labor statistics. When government provides misinformation, or mere personal opinion, as the truth, it harms the citizens it has sworn to protect.

The IQA is still part of the U.S. Code. Any president of the U.S. can immediately require federal agencies to provide the public with good-quality information. So far, no president since its enactment (Bush, Obama, Trump or Biden) has issued that order. As such, one can only conclude that the federal government's policy is to misinform and deceive the public.

It's time the federal government tells its citizens the truth about what it is doing. Without knowing the truth, it is impossible for citizens to know what they are getting for the money they send to Washington, other than enriching government officials and their friends. The federal government would be the beneficiary of the peoples' trust. Truth-telling is an essential function of government and its officials, unfortunately, it is lost to political decision-making.

CHAPTER 19

Prohibit Federal Gifts to Favored Groups

Since the beginning of the Republic, there has been a debate over the scope of Congress's power to spend our money and then tax us to generate more money to spend. James Madison argued Congress could only spend on the items enumerated in the Constitution. Alexander Hamilton argued the Constitution's Spending Clause is independent of the enumerated powers, thus allowing Congress to tax and spend as it deems necessary. The only limitation on congressional spending is that it must be for the general welfare.

Continuing to debate the limits of congressional spending is a waste of time. The Supreme Court clearly holds that Congress can spend on whatever it wants if it promotes the general welfare. Only Congress can make the determination of what is the general welfare.

Such a broad interpretation of Congress' ability to tax and spend has resulted in a massive expansion of government and a $34 plus trillion national debt to be accompanied by trillions in annual deficits for the next decade. This enormous debt will likely place our posterity in *de facto* involuntary servitude to the federal government. Our children will work to pay off our debt.

Most troubling, the general welfare has morphed from building the canals, bridges, and highways needed to make the U.S. an economic superpower into trillions of dollars in gifts to special interests and friends. These gifts to private entities include grants, tax credits, loan forgiveness, and paycheck protection plans.

A few examples of the cost of congressional gift giving:

- Between $721 billion and $1.2 trillion in annual grants to states as a bribe to manage many federal programs enacted outside the constitutional authority of Congress to legislate.
- $36 billion in grants to bailout poorly managed private sector union pension programs.
- Forgiving tens of billions of dollars of federal Paycheck Protection Program loans made to organizations controlled by the elite rich such as Paul Pelosi (husband of the Speaker of the House), Khloe Kardashian, Tom Brady, Reese Witherspoon, Forbes Media, Ruth Chris Steakhouse, The Washington Times, and more than a few members of Congress.
- $16 billion in farm aid was given to offset losses suffered by farmers on tariffs imposed on products sold to China. The top 10% of farmers receive 70% of the subsidies.

- The $330 billion prescription drug industry was granted $64 billion in federal research funding.
- Flood insurance subsidies are given to the wealthy to reduce the cost of insurance for high-end housing in flood-prone areas. This insurance program is potentially liable for $1.3 trillion in flood claims while only collecting $3.5 billion in annual premiums. The program has $25 billion in losses that taxpayers must pay.

In the most recent federal giveaway, the falsely named "Inflation Reduction Act," ("IRA"), Congress authorized $391 billion in new tax credits for corporations and individuals if they acquire green energy products or build green energy facilities. However, Goldman Sachs claims it will cost $1.2 trillion once the Biden administration changes congressional intent by issuing regulations that expand who qualify for the gifts. The administration is intentionally changing the scope of the law to satisfy climate and green activists without congressional approval. So much for Congress having the power of the purse.

The tax credits are to boost corporate sales of electric vehicles, the installation of rooftop solar panels, the development of solar power systems, heat pumps, water heaters, space heating, electric stoves, circuit breaker boxes, additional home insulation, and exterior windows, to name a few beneficiaries. These gifts are in addition to $577 billion in tax credits and grants for green energy projects since 2004.

Facilities that make batteries for electric vehicles are one of the biggest winners. Most electric battery factories will receive at least $1 billion, with the program costing over $200 billion. Unfortunately, however, the cost of each job created averaged $3.4 million while the workers holding those jobs are being paid $45,000.

The deceit surrounding tax credits is one of the prime reasons Congress cannot control spending. Tax credits are unlimited and exempt from the appropriations process. The credit goes to anyone who qualifies without any limit on the amounts the federal government can give away.

A week before the passage of the IRA, Congress authorized $280 billion to incentivize the semiconductor industry to build plants in the U.S. and invest in new research. The semiconductor industry is a $573 billion industry. It is expected to grow to $1.2 trillion by 2029 due to high product demand.

While there is almost no limit to Congress making gifts to its supporters and favored industries, historical precedents prohibited state governments from giving gifts to private entities. In the mid-1800s, many municipalities and states used public funds to purchase stock in the railroads built across the continent. Many of these governments lost or were swindled out of large amounts of taxpayer money. Forty-five states enacted similar constitutional limitations preventing gifts to private entities to prevent future losses. The limits placed on gifts to private parties came to be called "gift clauses."

The general gift clause prohibited state and local governments from giving or loaning public funds to private corporations or associations or for private undertakings. Initially, these provisions stopped government speculation with taxpayer money and the gifting of public funds to private entities for nonpublic purposes.

Over time, however, the courts began to legislate exceptions to the prohibitions for what they construed as a "public purpose," a purpose similar to the federal Constitution's general welfare clause. Courts have upheld legislation that makes gifts of public funds to a private entity if the gift would somehow result in a public benefit. The courts further expanded the definition of "public benefit" to include almost anything the legislature believes is a public benefit. Such gifts are found in almost all government projects, from parking lots to sports facilities, corporate rent subsidies, to outright gifts to attract business to a state or locality.

At the federal level, gifts are deemed legal to private parties for almost anything Congress wants to finance, incentivize, or throw money at. Taxpayer money flows, and the state and federal courts find it legal since the appropriations prove that the legislature viewed the gift to private parties as promoting the general welfare.

If a reasonable restructuring of the federal government is to occur, citizens must demand Congress enact a federal gift clause that prohibits giving taxpayer money to private sector entities. And while few believe that Congress will ever enact a prohibition on gifts to friends and interest groups, citizens must demand every person running for Congress take the following pledge:

"I pledge that, as a member of Congress, I will not vote to give, grant, or loan public funds or extend the public's credit to any private corporation, association, or private undertaking."

By asking every candidate for Congress to take this

pledge, citizens will easily distinguish between candidates seeking to protect the public's money and those seeking personal gain.

PART V

Rolling Back the Federal State
– Devolution of Power

CHAPTER 20

The Federal Government Is Too Big to Govern: The Case for Devolution

As noted in chapter 2, "There are times in the history of nations when the citizens of the nation need to act before those entrusted with the control and resources of the nation cause it harm. Now is the time for action!"

The historical events that fueled the growth of the federal government are many, including the Civil War, WWI, the Great Depression, WWII, the New Deal, the Great Society, several banking collapses, the financial crisis of 2008, the Fed's zero interest rate policy, the COVID-19 pandemic, the continuation of massive taxpayer subsidies years after the pandemic ended, and the Biden administration's extraordinarily delusional obsession with spending trillions on climate change.

The federal government has taken control of so many issues that it no longer has the time, expertise, and judgment to manage them. The federal government has morphed the nation's grand vision of exceptionalism into a state of unreason. It spends more than it can repay, regulates almost everything in commerce, always finds a pathway to war, and dispenses rights to anyone who feels harmed by anyone in society while prosecuting the honest people who raise families, go to school board meetings, attend church, and keep society running. It also opened its borders to any illegal immigrants who hire drug cartels to transport them to the U.S.

On the international front, U.S. power and prestige dissolves before the eyes of the public. The U.S. spends trillions on its intelligence operations but it was surprised by the 9/11 attacks. It is ignorant of the many terrorists coming into the country through its open southern border. Our well-funded intelligence operations even missed a Chinese spy balloon that was so large, people on the ground in Montana reported it to our government. Most recently, the brutal terrorists' attack by Hamas on Israel is another complete surprise to our trillion-dollar intelligence agencies. How unprepared can these intelligence agencies be and still protect the nation?

Our Constitution was structured to foster a strong economy while protecting citizens' freedom. Initially, the U.S. was established as a system of federalism in which power was divided between federal and state governments. The goal of the Constitution was to limit federal power. Unfortunately, the massive accumulation of federal power transformed the respective states into mere administrators of federal rule.

The federal government must devolve some of its many powers to the states to preserve the United States as a nation anchored in freedom. If the federal government does not allow the country to return to a viable structure of federalism that respects states as sovereigns, the U.S. will join the many nations that now hold the status of a "once-great power."

What is Devolution of Power?

Devolution transfers substantial power and authority from the federal government to state and local governments. Devolution differs from decentralization, which merely transfers certain functions from a central location to several locations. Decentralization would be a relevant concept if the federal government were to move its workforce out of Washington, DC.

Making devolution work and its benefits.

For devolution to work, the powers transferred to the states must include all powers necessary to implement the policies transferred, including decision-making authority, managerial control of the legal framework for the policies to be managed, and the ability to tax and spend. Moreover, the federal government must remove itself from managing the policies devolved to the states.

By assuming such powers, the states will have the capacity to implement all of the programs transferred to them by the federal government. States will also be able to eliminate current federal domestic programs unneeded, unaffordable, or unwanted by their citizens. Moreover, by clearly identifying the powers transferred, devolution allows the nation to operate as a unitary country that legally divides the management of issues between the federal government and the states for efficiency, and practical implementation of programs sought by citizens of the respective states. Devolution of power brings the government closer to the people it serves.

Greater program efficiency.

The programs administered by a state will be smaller in size and administered by a government that is closer to those it serves. By having more knowledge of the area and people served, the state and local governments administering the programs will be better able to achieve program goals. Greater efficiency results in more government account-ability for the services provided.

Enhances democracy.

In smaller communities, there is less bureaucracy. Participating in decision-making is more accessible and less costly. Greater participation in democracy builds trust in government. More people of ordinary means can seek elected office since the cost of local elections is far less than running for federal office.

Fosters innovation and trust.

With less bureaucracy to block innovative ideas, there is more focus on solutions and getting the job done than protecting the status quo. Since citizens are more trusting of and familiar with state and local government, they can better evaluate how the government manages the issues of most concern to them, such as health care, crime, and taxes. Significant citizen participation cannot happen when a distant central government lacks knowledge of the local issues yet controls the resolution of disputes.

Limits bureaucratic power.

Dividing power between authorities at different levels of government is an effective mechanism for deterring the ability of any government to become too powerful.

Assists with resolving conflicts.

Solutions are easier to achieve when there is an ability of citizens and government to exchange views.

Denationalizes controversial issues.

National governments nationalize all matters before them from abortion and education to local permitting, economic development and now the type of cars we can drive. When the federal government deals with state and local issues, the national lobbying organizations control the outcome to fit their national objectives. For example, it is the national environmental groups that block oil drilling and mineral mining in Alaska, not Alaskans. The same is true for oil and gas pipelines and forest management. National environmental groups control local development across the nation by capturing the federal bureaucracy. By allowing states to control controversial issues, each state will take a different path that is usually more satisfactory to the locals than the desires of the national groups. This approach allows citizens the ultimate right to live as they want and to vote with their feet by migrating to states that share their values.

The federal government will grow as much as it can. It will secure as much power as it can over any issue it can find a way to control. There is no limit to the government's lust to amass control over its people and resources. Unless restrained, the federal government will grow until it inflicts substantial harm on the people it is to serve. Once significant harm is inflicted on the nation, the government will cease, but likely so will the nation it governs. For this reason, if the federal government has any respect for the citizens of this nation, it must devolve a significant amount of its domestic power to the states, especially over social issues and economic development. The federal government must understand that, under our Constitution, it is not a supreme power that has sole control over the nation. Rather it holds the Constitution in trust for the people it governs.

The federal government must focus on the nation's defense and national issues. The states can very competently manage most domestic matters. Only by devolving power to the states and creating real federalism can the U.S. prevent authoritarian rule, a civil war, or a wholly weakened, unstable nation in a world of enemies.

CHAPTER 21

Options for Undertaking the Devolution of Power

The primary goal of devolving power is to enhance democracy by transferring many federal domestic powers to the lowest level of government that can effectively and efficiently manage the programs enacted to benefit its citizens. Devolution of power can only be achieved by concurrently limiting the federal government's power while enhancing the states' power. Devolving power will require the federal government to return many of the powers it has taken from the states over the last one hundred years. It will also require the states to determine which federal programs they want to manage and which programs are unneeded within their states. Since not all federal domestic programs are needed or wanted by each state, there will naturally be fewer government programs.

Devolution of power is essential if the respective states are to function as sovereigns rather than as administrators of federal programs. Devolution is necessary if the federal government is again to be a government of limited powers.

More importantly, devolution of power is essential if the federal government is to have the time and resources to focus on its most important responsibility - protecting the nation. There are several options for devolving federal power to the states.

Congress establishes an intergovernmental commission to identify the powers to be devolved to the states.

An intergovernmental commission made up of members of Congress and state governors and legislators would be the most straightforward and comprehensive way to approach this process. The Commission's task would be to identify all federally exercised powers that could be more efficiently and effectively managed by the states. It could start with the thousand-plus federal grants that entice states to implement programs the federal government often has no authority or resources to fully implement.

In 2022, the federal government awarded states $1.2 trillion in grants. The federal government collects these amounts from the states, and a portion of what the federal government collects or borrows from future generations in the form of more national debt is returned to the states to implement federal goals, not state priorities.

Without federal grants, states would likely stop implementing many of the federal programs. If a state wanted to enact a program similar to the eliminated federal program, it would tax its citizens to pay for the program. Since the federal government's commission on the taxes collected would be eliminated, it is likely the state could implement the former federal program for less than the combined federal/state contributions to fund the program.

Moreover, some states might terminate federal programs not deemed essential to them.

While the state commissioners will face federal resistance to returning any power to the states, the federal government will have to concede that some devolution of power must occur since its massive national debt will eventually force the federal government to discontinue funding existing state grant programs.

The federal grant programs are divided between welfare and regulatory programs. Currently 10 states, for fiscal reasons, refuse to accept federal money to expand state Medicaid programs under the Affordable Care Act. On regulatory issues, however, the respective states pay most of the cost of administering the federal programs. For instance, states administer 96.5% of the many federally delegated environmental programs, yet the federal grants fund only 28% of the programs' costs.

If numerous states refused to administer all federal regulatory programs, they would cause chaos as the federal government lacks the personnel to administer them without the help of the states. In retaliation, the federal government would likely refuse to issue federal permits for facilities operating in noncooperating states. States would have to sue the federal government, thus allowing the courts to determine the federal government's obligations to issue permits in non-cooperating states. It will be difficult for the federal government to prevail over state non-cooperation since the Supreme Court has been clear the federal government cannot commandeer state resources. Such a move by the states would also demonstrate that the federal government, without state cooperation, cannot manage or pay for the government it has created.

At some point, Congress would realize there must be serious negotiations over transferring federal powers to the states. When the work of the Commission is complete, its final product would be introduced in Congress and voted upon under rules established by Congress. The intergovernmental commission stands the best chance of success since the states would identify the programs they need and are likely to continue without money from Congress. Conversely, Congress would learn from the negotiations about the programs that are unwanted by the states and could eliminate those programs. Even if the intergovernmental commission fails, it will educate Congress and the states about the value of some programs and identify wasteful programs that can be eliminated.

Congress could enact a process similar to BRAC.

If Congress wants to avoid negotiations with the states and their legislatures, it could construct a Devolution of Power Commission comprised of experts to study and report on the federal programs most fitting to be managed by the states. It would be similar to the BRAC approach discussed in Chapter 13, but focused on federal programs rather than appropriations.

While the states would not be negotiating with Congress over the programs to be eliminated, they could make their views known through testimony and active lobbying. After receiving the BRAC type report and hearing the states' comments, Congress could allow the recommendations to go into effect unless it passes a Resolution of Disapproval that is signed by the president. Alternatively, it could allow amendments as it usually does for most legislation.

Re-constitute the Joint Committee to focus on the reduction of non-essential federal laws.

This new Joint Committee would be similar to the discussion of it in Chapter 13, however it would identify non-essential laws (not appropriations) for elimination. It would recommend to Congress the laws and programs to be eliminated. Such a process keeps all study and decision-making within Congress.

Once the recommendations are made, Congress could establish by rule that it must vote on the recommendations as a package. Alternatively, Congress could allow the recommendations to go through the regular order of committee hearings, markup, and floor debate. Once laws are eliminated, all of the regulations implementing those laws would be void.

Use of Interstate Compacts to devolve federal powers to the states.

Interstate compacts are cooperative actions between states to advance specific policies and programs. The compacts can be congressionally approved to ensure they have legal recognition or the compacts can be informal cooperation agreements between states to cooperate.

Formal, congressionally-approved compacts between states are established under Article I, sec.10, cl. 3 of the U.S. Constitution. These formal compacts range from boundary disputes to lotteries, river management, drivers' licenses, to multi-state tax matters. Ballotpedia provides a list of approved compacts from 1785 to 2018. Compacts can be on any subject that concerns several states. Every formal Compact requires congressional approval, which is very time-consuming. Due to approval complexities, States would be unlikely to submit and Congress would be unlikely to approve, enough formal Compacts to make a substantial difference in the devolution process. While the formal Interstate Compact approach is highly unlikely, it is an option that the states and Congress could utilize for the most significant issues that would grant federal legal status to multi-state cooperative agreements. Moreover, by having the approval of Congress, the Compact has more protection from legal challenge than an informal compact.

The Southern States Energy Compact is a workable example of the formal, congressionally approved Compact. It has eighteen members and was created to encourage economic development among its member states by improving energy, environmental, and technology policies. This compact has been an amazing success for bringing economic development to the South. The "[s]ix fastest growing states in the South now contribute more to the national GDP than the Northeast," the perennial powerhouse.

Under the informal Compact approach, the participating states would cooperate on specific programs without congressional approval. Congress could terminate informal compacts at any time, assuming Congress can secure the votes to repeal an agreement between states. A good example is the climate change compacts. States with similar policy views are organized into regional working units designed to regulate activities of regional concern. For example, nine states in the Northeast and Mid-Atlantic, and three west coast states, formed regional compacts to address climate concerns in a manner beyond what is allowed under federal law. The states entering these informal compacts initiated a cap-and-trade process that capped CO_2 emissions and authorized the trading of emission credits. The Environmental Protection Agency attempted such an approach with its Clean Power Plan. It was struck down by the U.S. Supreme Court for lack of congressional authority.

While the informal mechanism is an ad hoc approach to devolving power to the states, it could take several of the most controversial domestic issues off the federal plate, such as abortion, welfare, and illegal immigration, other than citizenship. The states in the various Compacts would address these issues uniformly, which will likely be dramatically different from existing federal policy. More importantly, this type of devolution gives the citizens of the respective states the freedom to elect the type of government they choose to live under.

Unfortunately, many Progressive activists will insist on federal control of the most controversial issues. Federal control gives the activists maximum power over policy issues nationwide. State control of policy issues gives local citizens maximum influence over a government closer to them. The informal Compact approach would be a compromise that allows a significant number of states to establish a uniform policy on controversial issues that are not federally regulated, e.g.; abortion, or to establish more restrictive policies than enacted by the federal government, e.g.; climate change. The downside of the informal compact is that it could be subject to legal challenge under the Dormant Commerce Clause as an interference with interstate commerce.

Congress could terminate all federal grants and unauthorized programs and authorize states to legislate in those areas.

The most drastic approach to devolving power to the states is for Congress to terminate all funding for all unauthorized federal programs and all grants to the states. Under House and Senate rules, Congress cannot fund unauthorized laws without waiving its rules. Second, many state grants are merely bribes to incentivize states to implement federal programs. Defunding these many programs could reduce the federal government's annual spending of $6 trillion by $1.7 trillion: $432 billion of unauthorized laws and $1.2 trillion in grants to states. Once Congress defunds specific programs, the states have complete control over areas defunded.

Congress has several viable options for devolving power to the states and substantially reducing federal spending. Congress needs the will and the wisdom to act while it still has time to get the nation's finances in order.

CHAPTER 22

Dividing the Powers Between the Federal Government and the States

If Congress agrees to devolve power to the states, the central question will be - which responsibilities are federal and which are state? While a division of responsibility will be determined by negotiation over what functions can be best managed by the federal government or the states, it is worth setting forth a few thoughts on what a division of responsibilities might be.

Federal powers.

The federal government must ensure all states have a Republican form of government. It would also have jurisdiction over all powers enumerated in the Constitution for the federal government to perform. The powers not enumerated and all implied powers would be the subject of the devolution of power negotiations.

The federal government would have exclusive control of the nation's common defense and foreign affairs, including military and intelligence operations, treaty negotiations, and international trade. On the domestic side, the enumerated powers include the many listed in Article I, section 8 of the U.S. Constitution.

As to the ability to regulate commerce, the Commerce Clause is unimaginably broad and the courts have expanded it so the federal government can regulate whatever it desires to control. If any federal powers are in need of being trimmed, it is the powers the courts have expanded by reliance on the Commerce Clause. Moreover, the implied powers granted to the federal government by the U.S. Supreme Court under the Dormant Commerce Clause rulings would also be subject to negotiations. A thesis on Constitutional law describes the relationship between the Commerce Clause and the Dormant Commerce Clause: "Although the Commerce Clause is framed as a positive grant of power to Congress and not an explicit limit on states' authority, the Supreme Court has also interpreted the Clause to prohibit state laws that unduly restrict interstate commerce even in the absence of congressional legislation—i.e., where commerce is dormant."

Moreover, since much of the federal government's power has been divined by the Supreme Court e.g., through the extensive application of the Necessary and Proper, General Welfare, and Spending clauses, those court-granted powers that greatly expand federal authority would also be subject in the negotiations. Since Congress should only regulate activities that have a direct and substantial impact on interstate commerce, the redistribution of these powers will be the primary focus of the negotiations.

What about Social Security, the expensive elephant in the room?

Due to the structure of Social Security, the tens of trillions collected by the federal government, the promises made to its many millions of recipients, and the fact that the federal government borrowed its excess funds for decades so it could overspend, the federal government must remain responsible for ensuring the program's viability. The good news is that Social Security is the easiest federal program to immediately fix. The many options include, raising the cap on the income taxed, eliminating the income cap altogether, increasing the percentage of payroll taxes paid by workers and employers, increasing the retirement age or some combination of the above to keep increases marginal.

State powers.

The respective states and local authorities would have exclusive responsibility for all police powers concerning the issues within their jurisdiction. Additionally, states would have exclusive jurisdiction over the federal lands returned to the states, and all abandoned federal lands and buildings in the respective states.

Additionally, the states would have exclusive responsibility over all education, consumer protection, highways, roads, the production and distribution of all forms of energy, environmental and labor policy, health care and health insurance, welfare, unemployment, job training, housing, economic development, and most other domestic programs.

Joint powers.

The federal and state governments would be jointly responsible for protecting the constitutional rights of every citizen. The federal government would have exclusive jurisdiction over the uniform rules for the naturalization of immigrants. The states, however, would regulate all other matters concerning immigration within the state, including the right to work and the receipt of state benefits, for example, education, welfare assistance, and a driver's license.

CHAPTER 23

State Legislatures: The Last Guardians of the Republic

Suppose Congress refuses to or cannot control an unresponsive federal government that is *de facto*, bankrupt, committing criminal acts and generally dysfunctional. Moreover, citizens fail to elect a sufficient number of members of Congress to serve as fiduciaries to check the power of the president. At that point, all efforts to devolve power to the states fail. The only remaining options rest with state legislatures as the last guardians of the Republic. States have several options for peacefully and legally challenging and changing an out-of-control federal government.

Calling for a Constitutional Convention to rebalance federal/state power.

The governing framework of the U.S. is intended to be federal/state federalism. Within this structure, power is balanced between the three branches of the federal government and between states and the federal government.

This power-sharing arrangement is designed to prevent any constitutional entity from gaining power beyond what the Constitution grants.

Unfortunately, the federal government has accumulated its massive power at the expense of the states for a century. To redistribute federal power, Article V of the Constitution empowers State legislatures with the right to amend the Constitution by calling for a Constitutional Convention.

While the states have never approved a Constitutional Convention, it remains the last best, viable option. Under Article V, upon application of the legislatures of two-thirds of the several states (34), Congress must call a Convention to propose Amendments to the Constitution. If the Convention's proposals are ratified by three-fourths of the states, those Amendments become part of our Constitution, notwithstanding the federal government's objections.

The state convention process cannot be denied, vetoed, or regulated by Congress, the president, or the governors of the respective states. The selected delegates control the Convention. If state legislatures honestly believe the federal government is not operating within the framework of our Constitution, it is their duty to act.

If a state initiated Constitutional Convention fails or the federal government obstructs it, the individual states must create legal mechanisms to protect the liberties of their citizens from federal tyranny. The state legislators must be cautious, peaceful, and act in complete compliance with federal laws; otherwise, the states will give the federal government the excuse it needs to use all powers under its control to crush the states and prosecute every participating citizen as an "enemy of the state," an insurrectionist, or as a terrorist. It is likely martial law will be imposed on the offending states. State mechanisms for challenging federal obstructions to liberty are:

Non-Cooperation.

Martin Luther King, Jr. used non-violence and non-cooperation to secure equal justice for all in the United States. Gandhi used these tactics to topple the British Empire. The States wanting to protect the constitutional rights of their citizens could, as a group, voluntarily take a non-cooperation stance on federal programs.

States and local governments currently participate in over a thousand federal programs and administer most major domestic programs, e.g., hazardous waste, water pollution, labor, education, Medicaid, and child nutrition. These grant programs allow the federal government to control state domestic programs as the price for the grant money. The states would merely refuse to administer any federal programs. While a few states, at times, refuse federal funds to administer unwanted programs such as Medicaid, these few refusals do not impact the overall federal regulatory efforts to control state activities.

Should a large group of states, twenty or more, refuse to implement many of the federal programs, the federal government would need to negotiate with the states on a power-sharing arrangement if it sincerely wants its programs administered. If the federal government refuses to negotiate, it loses control over the many federal programs run by the states, or it must manage those programs in the non-cooperating states, which would require thousands more employees at a substantially greater cost than it currently pays the states.

States can protect citizens when the federal government abandons its constitutional responsibilities.

President Biden has opened the Southern border of the United States to illegal immigration, criminal cartels, and foreign terrorists. Biden's unreason has allowed upwards of five million people into this country illegally since he was inaugurated. The border states have appealed for help from the federal government. The federal government has ignored their pleas for two years, notwithstanding the illegal immigrants present a tremendous financial burden to states and local communities, overwhelm local schools and take up such a significant number of beds in hospitals that they deprive local citizens of medical care. The worst impact of the open borders is that the drug cartels inflicted 75,000 fentanyl overdose deaths on Americans just in 2022. Several governors and mayors consider the harm caused by this massive illegal entry of foreigners into the U.S. to be the equivalent of an invasion.

Congress has the power to establish a uniform rule of naturalization, and the president is obligated to protect each state from invasion. Both institutions have abdicated their responsibilities.

To protect its citizens, the Texas legislature enacted a law that makes illegal entry into the state from a foreign nation a crime. The first offense is a misdemeanor, and the second offense of unlawful entry is a felony. The law authorizes state and local police the power to arrest illegal migrants and grants state court judges the ability to issue orders to remove the illegals to Mexico.

The Texas law is highly controversial. Opponents claim the U.S. Supreme Court ruled in 2012 that the federal government preempted an Arizona law that makes it a crime to be unlawfully present in the U.S.

Texas, however, makes the illegal entry from a foreign nation at any point of entry other than a lawful point of entry the crime, not the mere presence in the U.S. While the U.S. Supreme Court will likely decide the case years from now, the situation with illegal immigration since 2012 has gotten dramatically worse.

In 2012, there were 364,768 apprehensions of illegals. In 2022 there were 2,214,652 identified apprehensions of illegals. In December 2023, illegal border crossing was the highest ever, exceeding 225,000 in one month. At that point, the Governor of Texas declared a state of invasion and constructed a razor wire fence at Eagle Pass, Texas to block future illegal immigration. The Biden administration ordered Governor Abbott of Texas to remove the razor wire. He refused. It is now a standoff between the federal government and Texas. The issue is whether the governor of a state has the power under the U.S. Constitution to protect the citizens of the state he governs when the federal government refuses to protect them, notwithstanding the president having a constitutional duty to protect states from invasion.

While this controversy will present several issues to the Supreme Court, the critical issue will be the right of a state to protect itself when the federal government abandons its constitutional obligation to protect the state from millions of people crossing illegally into it, an act that many consider an invasion. The Supreme Court's decision on this issue will set the stage for enacting new Personal Liberty laws or it could become the flash point for dismantling the Republic. All rests on Article IV, section 4 of the U.S. Constitution.

Develop a 21st century version of State Personal Liberty laws.

From the founding of the Republic to the Civil War, abolitionists persuaded states to enact Personal Liberty laws to protect fugitive slaves. These laws were grounded on the principle that sovereign states have the power to protect individuals within their borders. To avoid federal supremacy rendering inconsistent state laws void, the States enacted laws making it difficult for bounty hunters to capture fugitive slaves by denying them state resources, e.g., bounty hunters could not hold fugitive slaves in local jails. Moreover, the imposition of high court costs to secure the "legal transfer" of a fugitive slave substantially reduced the value of the bounty.

Today, to maneuver around the Supremacy Clause, states could enact laws expanding the civil rights of those living in a state. Washington State has enacted stronger protections against warrantless searches than the federal Constitution. Eight blue states and hundreds of cities have enacted Sanctuary laws to protect immigrants from federal prosecution. One state proposes prohibiting federal law enforcement officers from arresting or detaining individuals solely based on a civil immigration detainer. On the "red" side of the ledger, three states and over 230 counties in 19 states have enacted Sanctuary laws to protect the constitutional rights of gun owners.

The most widespread use of Personal Liberty laws is found in states that have legalized marijuana, a substance illegal under federal criminal law. The number of states legalizing marijuana increases every time a state legislature is in session. Moreover, no uniform law governs it, so each state has different standards, making it difficult to categorize the laws. The most straightforward breakdown is twenty-three states and the District of Columbia have legalized it. In another fifteen states, it is legal for medical use. It is illegal in twelve states. The marijuana laws illustrate that states cannot be forced to implement federal law if they act in groups. Moreover, by decriminalizing marijuana, the states expand personal freedom in light of federal prohibitions. If the federal government wants marijuana laws enforced throughout the nation, it will have to implement them itself, which it cannot or is unlikely to do.

Today, the federal government attacks the constitutional rights of the objectionable in the areas of free speech, religious freedom, and freedom of association by its illegal spying on Americans, and its unequal application of the law, referred to as a two-tier justice system.

New types of Personal Liberty laws are needed to protect citizens in the 21st century from unjust federal actions, just as those types of laws protected fugitive slaves from bounty hunters. States can protect their citizens by making it a crime for federal officials to violate state civil rights statutes. Areas of enhanced protection might include prohibiting warrantless spying on American citizens, criminalizing the filing of false documents to mislead courts so federal officials can prosecute innocent Americans, and making the imprisonment of citizens for long periods without a trial a state crime. Moreover, Personal Liberty laws could make the systematic enforcement of a two-tier justice system a violation of state civil rights laws. These additional state protections are necessary since the federal government refuses to prosecute the crimes committed by federal officials against the objectionable. The findings of the *Horowitz and Durham reports* on DOJ and FBI corruption establish that the two agencies have violated federal law. Yet, the federal government ignores the crimes committed by federal officials.

As states attempt to restrain federal criminal activity within their states, the federal government will assert its agents and itself are immune from prosecution under sovereign immunity and the Supremacy Clause of the Constitution.

The assertion of these immunity defenses to the commission of state crimes raises the most threatening aspects of federal rule over the nation. What is the impact on the Republic if the federal government refuses to prosecute itself or its agents for violations of federal criminal law and is granted immunity for violations of state criminal law?

It is likely that if a few states enacted State Liberty laws, one or more of the states would indict federal officials for violating state criminal law. When the federal government raises its immunity defenses, it will have to establish, under the U.S. Supreme Court's precedent in *In Re Neagle*: (1) its agents were authorized to perform their actions under federal law, and (2) that their actions were necessary and proper to fulfilling their federal duties.

Absent a federal law authorizing federal criminal activity in the states, the case will proceed into legal discovery to determine the facts surrounding the government's conduct. The litigation will force the DOJ/FBI and other agencies to explain their conduct, produce supporting documentation to justify their actions, identify the agency's decision-making process, and produce the agency orders initiating its actions. This legal discovery will subject federal police and investigative agencies to public scrutiny and liability. Such exposure is necessary if the federal government is to be, in any manner, held accountable for its illegal actions.

Eventually, the federal/state conflicts under the Personal Liberty laws will force the U.S. Supreme Court to decide whether states can hold federal officials responsible for violating state criminal law. If the federal government can order and/or ignore violations of federal criminal law by its officials and obtain immunity for violations of state criminal law, the federal government renders the Constitution irrelevant. A Supreme Court decision on the validity of state Personal Liberty laws and the federal government's compliance or non-compliance with that decision will determine whether the Republic exists in more than name only.

CHAPTER 24

How It All Ends Is an Either/Or Situation

Since politicians want more government, money, and resources, the federal government will never voluntarily limit its quest for power. It will hold onto power until the collapse is inevitable. These actions are always a mistake since they leave the citizens they are to serve in chaos and sometimes worse – in poverty, civil disorder, and perhaps war. History is replete with examples of failed empires. If this happens in the U.S., there will be dark times ahead. The federal government's current mismanagement of the United States will be the spark that ignites its 1433 moment.

If the citizens of the United States fail to elect fiduciaries to run the federal government, and a Constitutional Convention fails or is obstructed by the federal government, the only hope for preserving the Republic rests with the states and state legislatures. Initially, certain states will attempt to persuade the federal government that it is mismanaging the nation and causing it to collapse. The federal government will arrogantly reject all state proposals. At that point, the states will be forced to choose between servitude to the federal government and protecting the constitutional freedoms of their citizens. Every state that joins the cause of promoting and protecting freedom will add to the collective freedom of the nation.

There should be no surprise that more than a few states will choose servitude, believing the federal government will tax the nation so it can continue supporting the states in servitude. The servitude states will be disappointed. Federal taxation has limits. Only so much money can be taken from citizens or printed by the government until citizens and the world render the dollar worthless. Federal power also has limits. There are only so many unreasonable mandates that citizens can be forced to obey absent the use of force.

As the U.S. appears militarily and economically weaker to the world, there will be insurmountable challenges to the United States by a competing superpower or a combine of regional powers. The federal government will be hesitant, confused and unable to seriously confront the challenges.

While the future is never written, the future of a nation is generally determined by the quality of persons elected to manage it and the intensity of the people's loyalty to the nation. In the United States, the federal government, unfortunately, rules without having the trust of 80% of its citizens. The arrogant federal officials have separated themselves from the citizens. The federal government believes it is the ruler and citizens are merely commodities that pay taxes.

Only when those managing the federal government understand that they manage a government of limited powers for the benefit of the people can they begin to put the nation on a stable footing. Once the federal government recognizes it cannot manage all the matters it seeks to control, negotiations can begin over what powers can be devolved to the states. The negotiations will attempt to rebalance the allocation of governing responsibilities between the federal government and the states. Both governments need each other to help manage and protect a complex society.

By creating a federal government that focuses on protecting national security and the nation's economic well-being while empowering states to manage most of the domestic needs of their citizens, the nation begins to restore accountability and trust in government. Devolution of power to the states may be the only viable path that citizens and states can organize around to save the Republic. All the political paths that increase federal power seem bent on destroying the nation.

While electing fiduciaries and devolving federal domestic powers to the states may seem impossible, it is far easier than rebuilding a collapsed nation burdened with massive debt, regulatory sclerosis, continuous wars, and little concern for the average American.

In the final analysis, the citizens of the U.S. must understand they are responsible for their government and what it does. Citizens do not have the "just following orders" defense since they elect the individuals who manage their government. The citizens of the U.S. are now confronted with an "either/or" situation. Either citizens elect a government of fiduciaries that limit the power of the federal government, or they must accept living in an all-powerful, federal state that is organized around corruption, deception, and eventually brutal tyranny.

As the Grand Duke Mikhailovich told the last Czar of Russia before the revolution:

> *A situation like this cannot last long.*

ABOUT THE AUTHOR

William L. Kovacs has forty-five years of hands-on experience grappling with the most complex aspects of federal policy. He served as a chief counsel on Capitol Hill, a senior vice president for the U.S. Chamber of Commerce, chairman of a state environmental board, and a partner in D.C. law firms. He testified forty times before Congress and participated in several hundred federal rulemakings. The author knows first-hand how Washington manipulates policy to benefit political friends, not citizens.

His first book, *Reform the Kakistocracy*, received the 2021 Independent Press Award for Social/Political Change. He is the 2019 recipient of the Albert Nelson Marquis Lifetime Achievement Award by Marquis Who's Who.

Polls show only 20% of citizens trust the U.S. federal government to do what is right most of the time. Polls find the average American believes the nation is two-thirds of the way to "the edge of a civil war." Can the federal government unite and govern this polarized nation? If not, how does it divide?

Devolution of Power directly addresses these questions. It provides a roadmap to unwinding the massive accumulation of federal power by returning many domestic functions to the states. By distributing power throughout the nation, the federal government can focus on protecting America while empowering citizens in the respective states with the freedom to determine the domestic policies they want to be implemented by more efficient governments closer to them.

Unlike many books on government reform, *Devolution of Power* is not just a list of complaints that leave the reader seeking solutions. It addresses how to restructure a federal government before it collapses the nation:

- Rekindling the idea that government officials must serve as fiduciaries, not self-interested politicians.
- Providing alternative mechanisms for rolling back federal power.
- Outlining a restructuring plan to devolve federal power to the states.
- Identifying options for trimming the national debt and the federal bureaucracy.
- Describing the character traits needed by elected officials to restore trust in government.

While electing fiduciaries and devolving federal domestic powers to the states may seem to be an impossible task, the author presents a compelling case that it is a far easier task than rebuilding a collapsed nation burdened with massive debt, regulatory sclerosis, continuous wars, and little concern for the average American.

Paperback-Press

ISBN 9781960499790

90000

9 781960 499790

Stéphane Ternoise

faire Ségolène Royal - Olivier Falorni

ce qu'il faut en retenir pour l'Histoire

Un écrivain engagé,

un observateur indépendant

Jean-Luc Petit éditeur